In Other Words

In Other Words

Dominique Enright

Michael O'Mara Books Limited

First published in 2005 by

Michael O'Mara Books Limited

9 Lion Yard

Tremadoc Road

London SW4 7NQ

A CIP catalogue record for this book is available from the British Library.

ISBN 1-84317-144-9

1 3 5 7 9 10 8 6 4 2

Designed and typeset by Burville-Riley

Printed and bound in England by Clays Ltd, St Ives plc

www.mombooks.com

Contents

Acknowledgements

Of the sources mentioned in the final section of this book ('Useful Books and Websites'), I am indebted to R. W. Holder's *Oxford Dictionary of Euphemisms: How Not to Say What You Mean* and to the contributors to *Wikipedia*, the excellent online encyclopedia.

Thanks are due, too, as always, to all at Michael O'Mara Books, especially Kate Gribble for her patience and forbearance. I am also indebted to Blacksheep Design for the cover design, and to Marc Burville-Riley for the book's interior.

Dominique Enright, 2005

Introduction

Do you call a spade a spade? Or do you mince your words? Are you mealy-mouthed and circumlocutory, or are you brutally direct? Are you vulgar or precious? Harsh or kind? Politically correct (what have politics got to do with it?) or offensive? Do you blaspheme and utter profanities? Or are you polite and genteel? Do you always say what you mean? Do you always mean what you say? The chances are that you will answer both yes and no to most if not all of these questions – the majority of us temper our language and choice of words to the occasion and to the individuals concerned. What is surprising is how imprecise the words we choose are.

'The true use of speech is not so much to express our wants as to conceal them': the writer Oliver Goldsmith (1730–1774) could have added that although we might be concealing our wants, we often still want them to be recognized. What is more, the concealment has the added advantage, on occasion, of giving us an escape route – our meaning having been effectively obfuscated, we can, if necessary, claim, or at least allow the doubt to persist, that the other party has 'not quite understood' (even when they have).

Euphemism is just one of a group of figures of speech that have developed as language has evolved, and have become more sophisticated as humans have become increasingly complicated. While most metaphors and similes, for example, serve to specify the speaker's meaning and perhaps also to indicate the speaker's feelings about what he or she is talking about, euphemisms – which, to add to the confusion, are also metaphors – tend to work by implication, or by a hope that your interlocutor understands what it is that you're saying, without your actually saying it. Closely related, often overlapping – indeed, they are all forms of euphemism – are genteelisms (usually long or foreign words that are held to be so much less coarse), weasel words, doublespeak, politically correct terminology (now there's a minefield), circumlocution, taboo deformation, slang (including Cockney rhyming slang), tropes, evasion, periphrasis, neologism, propaganda, Newspeak, dysphemisms (which are neutral or mildly rude terms, often comic) and cacophemisms (when one is deliberately offensive). More could be added to this list, but as their meanings already overlap or coincide (as tropes are metaphors, and periphrasis is circumlocution), to list any more would be tautology or even pleonasm (the use of more words than are necessary to convey meaning). The English language has so many words to describe aspects of itself …

The word 'euphemism' is from the Greek roots *eu* and *pheme*, meaning to speak auspiciously or to speak well; it was, and still is, applied to taboo subjects such as sex, death and religion. For centuries, it has been deemed wise not to offend the gods for fear of unreasonable reprisals, and this sensitivity resulted in the very earliest euphemisms. In ancient Greece, for example, the Erinyes or Furies (terrifying goddesses of 'justice', who persecuted malefactors) became the Eumenides, the 'Kindly Ones'. (Those who are interested in words might like to note that 'Eumenides' has the prefix 'eu', indicating 'good' and 'auspicious', as have 'Eucharist', 'eulogy', 'euphemism', 'eupeptic', etc.; the 'eu' of 'eunuch', though, is from *eune*, meaning 'bed'.)

The euphemism's origins establish it as a mild term to be used in the place of one considered taboo and therefore not to be articulated. Yet it has since been extended to stand in for any term regarded as offensive, distasteful, blunt, indelicate, upsetting, embarrassing, vulgar or demeaning. In some cases the extension has been carried too far and has become the object of ridicule and satire – as in some politically correct language. Also by extension, but in another direction, a new, euphemistic term might be coined to hide not objectionable words but unpleasant ideas – spin doctors (a dysphemism for spokesmen, sorry, spokespersons … or a euphemism for propagandists) like to use these kinds of euphemisms to soothe the electorate. 'Job seekers', for instance, sounds so much more positive than 'the unemployed'. Trades, professions, organizations and institutions have all developed their own euphemistic language, designed to persuade or placate the public: 'technicians', 'engineers' and 'operatives' abound in the territory of what is, let's face it, no more than menial labour, while poky flats are 'bijou residences', and when the army 'goes in' there is, rather than civilian deaths and injuries, something called 'collateral damage' – which sounds reassuringly like nothing worse than a few broken windowpanes. For these reasons and for its mealy-mouthedness, the euphemism is frequently scoffed at – 'why not call a spade a spade?' its detractors ask. And certainly there is much to criticize in the use of euphemism – euphemistic speech is often woolly and misleading, or exasperatingly prim and priggish, evasive, long-winded or plain ridiculous. A fairly recent development is that of the 'stylish' word, a form of genteelism without genteelism's prim connotations. Thus it is trendier to suffer from 'catarrh' than the common cold; your condition will 'ameliorate' rather than improve, and you might reside in a 'cottage' rather than live in a small house.

On the other hand, euphemism, in presenting an acceptable vocabulary, has enabled many to discuss or at least refer to things they would otherwise not feel able even to mention. Euphemism can avoid hurting feelings or religious sensibilities; euphemism saves many a face and boosts many an ego by replacing a term with shameful or embarrassing connotations with one that is more positive and encouraging. Sometimes, a carefully chosen euphemism can, rather than mislead, actually pinpoint the speaker's meaning, indeed reveal more about the speaker than was ever intended. And finally, euphemisms have hugely enriched our vocabulary, offering a colourful array of alternative terms to choose from. It is by no means time for the euphemism to be 'downsized' (a euphemism for 'sacked' or 'fired' – words which are themselves dysphemisms for 'dismissed from employment').

Like language itself, euphemisms change over time. They might fall into disfavour or even come to be considered objectionable. For example, 'crippled' gave way to the kinder 'handicapped', which subsequently was deemed too negative and was replaced with 'disabled' (which seems to mean exactly the same thing but without the golfing connotations to liven it up). 'Disabled' itself is now in the process of a wash-and-brush-up, as – according to some – it could be taken to mean that a disabled person is unable to do anything at all, i.e. that they have been 'turned off', like a computer application (idle thought: will 'disabled' come to stand for 'dead'?). Any sensible person knows this not to be the case, but then sense rarely gets a look-in – and thus the term 'differently abled' is making its appearance: never mind that this suggests that the 'differently abled' person can do things that most people cannot do. (Cannot walk but can fly? In a discussion such as this it is difficult to be politically correct – at least without disabling any sense of perspective.) 'Differently abled' would be fine if it were true, but its intended meaning is that while the person in question is able to do some of the things that the more fortunate majority can do, there are a few things that, unfortunately, he or she is unable to do, for whatever physical or mental reasons – 'unable' being the key word here.

In other cases, a euphemism might come to seem over-refined to some and not genteel enough for others. Step forward euphemisms for 'lavatory' (itself a euphemism). At some point, 'lavatory' was considered not 'polite' enough for society, so a replacement euphemism was found for it – 'toilet' (which carries the same meaning of 'washing'). In the US especially, however, this word has been found too obvious (after all, we all know what he's gone in there to do), so 'toilet' is replaced by 'bathroom' (even though we know he's not having a bath) or 'restroom' (rest? He's only just got up), or even 'comfort station' (eh?), and so on. At the same time, the 'word rebels' are protesting against the genteelism of 'toilet' (and are not over happy with 'lavatory', though they'll tolerate 'loo') – so along comes 'bog', and so it goes. In the meantime, everybody has lost sight of the original term ... if the room in question ever had one. Dr Seuss wraps it up nicely in the animated film, *It's Grinch Night!*, in which a child goes 'to the euphemism'.

In the pages that follow you will find a selection of euphemisms (and cousins of euphemisms) covering the life and culture of both past times and the present day, of the coarse and the refined, the religious and the commercial. From lavatories to liquidation by way of lasciviousness, and from death to drunkenness via doo-doos, you will come across expressions you know well, euphemisms that you use even without realizing that they are euphemisms, and others that, perhaps, you did not know. Euphemisms are by their very nature changeable and evasive, but here you will find some enlightenment and even some facts. You will be reminded of the origins of such harmless exclamations as 'Gosh!', 'Gee whiz!' and 'Sugar!'; why you should know that a spade is a digging tool and a lady of the night is no better than she should be; what might happen when you mention the devil; why most people bump their heads on glass ceilings rather than rise through them; what happens on a one-way ride; and why you don't want to be street pizza or have the Sandy McNabs.

This does not pretend to be a comprehensive survey of euphemisms – indeed, you will doubtless think of many not included in these pages – but, rather, it is a somewhat eclectic selection that aims to inform and to amuse.

Glossary

Buzzword
a technical word or phrase, often a neologism, that has become fashionable; can be used euphemistically.

Cacophemism
an intentionally harsh word or expression instead of a polite one; at face value the opposite of a euphemism, it is often used as a euphemism, a coarse word sometimes being less embarrassing than the proper term.

Circumlocution
literally to 'speak around' the subject, using a phrase that implies the subject without mentioning it; this can sometimes take the form of a little 'story' which becomes established as a euphemism. Everyone, for instance, knows what people mean when they say they are 'going to see a man about a dog'.

Doublespeak
generally the deliberate use of neutral terms to disguise actions which might give rise to concerted objection – a device much used by governments and military organizations.

Dysphemism
similar to cacophemism, but less offensive and sometimes just humorous. Those who automatically sneer at euphemisms as being genteel or misleading might take note. For example, 'bog' or 'bog house' for 'lavatory'.

Euphemism

a substitute word or phrase used instead of the correct term in order to make the subject more palatable to the listener, and, possibly, less awkward or embarrassing for the speaker. Most if not all of the terms listed in this book can be used as euphemisms.

Evasion

the use of a word or phrase which implies what you do mean, without actually meaning that (e.g. 'unmarried' to mean 'homosexual' or abstractions such as 'the situation'), or simply to avoid saying anything definite at all ('er … you know …')

Genteelism

a word or phrase thought by its user to be more refined than the 'correct' term, which is considered coarse or vulgar. Genteelisms often take the form of foreign or longer words (e.g. 'proceeding' for 'going') or non-specific terms like 'private parts'.

Metaphor

a figure of speech in which a word or phrase is used to describe or refer to something to which it is not applicable.

Neologism

a newly coined word or expression, not necessarily a euphemism; doublespeak terms, however, such as 'collateral damage', 'downsize', and politically correct terms are often neologisms as well as euphemisms.

Newspeak

the fictional language in George Orwell's *Nineteen Eighty-Four* has its real-life equivalents in doublespeak and the kind of politically correct terminology used in propaganda.

Periphrasis
the use of circumlocution.

Political correctness
a well-intentioned policy that involves avoiding any terms that might seem unjust, give rise to discrimination or cause offence. The substitute term attempts to be affirmative or at least negatively negative. This has led to much confusion and much mockery.

Propaganda
biased or one-sided information used to promote a particular – usually political – cause or point of view; this can often comprise doublespeak and euphemism. (In some countries, however, it means no more than commercial advertising, which is the same thing but a weaker form of it.)

Slang
informal language, often used as euphemism, especially in respect of taboo subjects such as sex. It comes in various forms, including rhyming slang, which is also often used as euphemism.

Taboo deformation
distortion of taboo words: 'sugar' for 'sh*t', 'gee whiz' for 'Jesus', and so on.

Trope
a metaphorical use of a word or expression.

Weasel words
generalizations or intentionally vague statements; these can be euphemisms, for instance when they are used in order not to give offence – or to lay the blame on someone else ('Some people think you took the wrong move …').

To do with religion and superstition

Religion

The majority of euphemisms – or at least alternative expressions – found in relation to religion are today comparatively mild swear words or exclamations. Blasphemy – profane or sacrilegious talk about God and sacred things – once included (and still does to an extent) the irreverent use of the name of God ('Thou shalt not take the name of the Lord thy God in vain'). The word 'God' is in a sense a euphemism as the entity referred to is a god – the only god, admittedly, but God is not his name; he is also called Lord, but Lord is not his name. In the Hebrew biblical texts he is called Yahweh (Jehovah) because, as God's name came to be regarded as too sacred for expression, the consonants JHVH or JHWH, possibly from the Hebrew verb *hawah* or *hajah*, meaning 'is', together with vowels taken from the word 'Adonai' ('Lord'), came to be used in the place of the name that could not be uttered. 'Allah', also used as a 'name' for the one eternal, omniscient, omnipotent God, has similarly vague origins. In all cases, to be on first-name terms with a deity would be considered overfamiliar, to say the least. To voice the stand-in term 'God' in even the mildest of curses or interjections was once beyond the pale, and even today euphemistic forms of 'God', 'Jesus', 'hell' etc. are used in preference – 'for the Lord will not hold him guiltless that taketh his name in vain', continues the Third Commandment.

These euphemistic forms generally take the shape of 'taboo deformation' and 'minced oaths', in which the pronunciation and spelling of the word or phrase are altered. 'Minced oaths' – where you minced, or cut up, your words – developed during the sixteenth to eighteenth centuries as part of the Puritan culture of the Protestant Reformation. Over time they have come to seem somewhat comical, and to the modern ear or eye tend to carry connotations of swashbuckling heroes, moustachioed villains and Georgette Heyer romances. The modern corruptions of sacred names, which have proliferated in the US in particular (gee whiz, etc.), by and large have the equally harmless flavour of Disney or *Tom and Jerry*.

It is interesting to note that euphemisms for the same word are often not interchangeable, hinting at different circumstances and emotions. Thus you might exclaim 'Jeez!' in exasperation, but 'Cripes' when startled and 'Crikey' when impressed.

In the list which follows there are comparatively few euphemisms for the Devil, as use of his name would not in most cases be blasphemous, so much as inviting trouble. For that reason his alternative names have been listed under Superstition. Following here are all the well-known euphemisms – many still in regular use today – which take their roots in religion.

Begorra(h)
    by God, generally seen as Irish.

Bejabbers
    by Jesus, from 'Bejaysus'.

Bejaysus
    by Jesus, Irish – and when uttered in a strong Irish accent it
    is hardly a deformation.

Blazes
    hell, as in 'What the blazes?' or 'He can go to the blazes!'.

Bleeding heck
    bloody hell.

Blimey
    (God) blind me.

Blinking heck
    bloody hell.

Bloody
    once itself taboo, said to be from 'by Our Lady', supposedly
    Mary, mother of God.

By George
    by God.

By Gum
    by God.

By Jove
    by God (Jove, the most powerful Roman deity, as substitute).

Cheese 'n' Rice
    Jesus Christ.

Cheesus
    Jesus.

Chrissakes
    '(for) Christ's sake' – hardly a disguise.

Cor blimey
    God blind me.

Crikey

Christ.

Criminy

Christ, a seventeenth-century 'minced oath', the sound of the word perhaps suggested to its instigators by the Italian *crimine* for crime. ('Crimini, jimini! Did you ever hear such a nimminy pimminy Story as Leigh Hunt's *Rimini*?': Byron, 1816.) See also 'Jiminy Cricket'.

Cripes

Christ.

Dang

(God) damn.

Dangnabbit, dangnation

damnation.

Darn, durn

(God) damn.

Darnation

damnation.

Deuce

the devil (in spite of the similarity to *deus*, 'god'); probably seventeenth century and possibly ultimately deriving from the Latin *duos*, with specific reference to throwing two aces in a dice game (that being the worst throw).

Dickens

as in 'What the dickens?' – a reference to the devil, probably sixteenth century, so nothing to do with the Victorian novelist.

Dog

anagram of God, rare and blasphemous.

Doggone

God damned, mostly US.

Drat

probably from the seventeenth-century minced oath ''od rat it' for 'God rot it'.

Egad

minced oath – 'a God' for 'by God'.

For crying out loud

for Christ's sake (which could also be a way of hinting at 'f**k' or sanitizing said four-letter word after uttering it: 'F**k... rying out loud').

Gad

fifteenth-century deformation of 'God', hardly subtle.

Gadzooks

God's hooks, seventeenth-century minced oath referring to the nails that held Jesus to the cross.

Gawd

a more recent obvious deformation of 'God'.

Gee

Jesus or Jerusalem.

Gee whiz

Jesus.

Goddam, Goddamn, Goddarn

God damn(ed).

Goldang

as 'Goddam'.

Goldarn

as 'Goddam'.

Golly

God – a simple case of taboo deformation.

Golly gee

God Jesus (as in 'Jesus God!').

Goodness gracious
good God.
Good grief
good God.
Good/goodness gracious
good God.
Gorblimey
God blind me.
Gosh
God.
Gosh darn/ed
God damn/ed.

Heck
hell (which might be prefixed with 'flaming' or 'flipping' –
i.e. 'f**king').
Hot place, the
hell (not an oath).

Jeepers Creepers
Jesus Christ.
Jeez
Jesus.
Jiminy Cricket
Jesus Christ. The expression precedes the Disney character
by centuries. With various spellings, among them jimini,
gemony, gemini, the expression is thought to derive
from a corruption of *Jesu Domine* – 'Jesus Lord'. In William
Congreve's 1695 play *Love for Love*, the character Miss Prue
exclaims: 'O Gemini! Well, I always had a great mind to tell
lies; but they frighted me, and said it was a sin.'
Jumping Jehoshaphat
'jumping Jesus' or 'jumping Jehovah', 'jumping' for the sake
of alliteration.

Lord of the Flies
 the devil; Beelzebub, 'fly-lord' in Hebrew.

My goodness
 my God.

Od, Odd
 God (minced oath).
Odds-bodkins
 God's sweet body (minced oath).
Old Nick
 the devil (see under Superstition).
Other place, the
 hell, the place that is not heaven (not an oath).

'Sblood
 God's blood.
'Sdeath
 God's death (minced oath).
'Strewth
 God's truth (a nineteenth-century contraction).

Tarnation
 damnation (a variation of 'darnation').

Zounds
 God's wounds (i.e. Jesus Christ's), a minced oath from the
 sixteenth or seventeenth century.

Superstition

Like religious euphemisms, the following euphemistic terms are
inspired by a desire to appease, or at least avoid provoking, a
supernatural being. In the case of religion, euphemism is used in

an attempt to avoid blasphemy (which would incur the wrath of God); with superstition it stems from the simple belief that we are surrounded by inimical beings who will 'get us' if we step out of line. Thus the drought that causes the crops to fail is not an accident of the weather, but is a punishment by malicious gods or sprites for some offence unwittingly given. One way to avoid offending someone is to avoid any reference to them, and so we call these beings – fairies, demons, whatever they may be – by some alternative name or descriptive phrase (which is not necessarily always an accurate description). To be on the safe side, these descriptive phrases sometimes imply goodness or nobility in the thing or being in question, when such a characteristic is in actuality its very antithesis.

The devil is an especially tricky customer as you only have to mention him ('talk of the devil') and he will turn up, an uninvited and most unwelcome guest. So he is – or rather was – referred to by all manner of names or phrases, the assumption being that they would be understood by all right-minded people, without actually summoning Satan himself.

Auld
see under 'old'. Dialect or rural accents are, like foreign words, seen as adequate substitutes for the actual word.

Bad fire, the
hell – safer not to mention hell itself in case the devil pops up.

Bad man, the
the devil.

Black lad, the
(also, among many others, black man, black prince, black Sam, black spy, black thief etc.) the devil. The devil is associated with black, darkness, and also blackness as in night – the time for dark deeds and nefarious activities, all

pursued under cover of darkness. (Any reference to the devil as 'the black man' would have been made with no thought of racial issues.) But as well as this he was traditionally thought to enter a house by way of a soot-filled chimney and blackened fireplace – just like Father Christmas – and so the name arises from this too.

Bog(e)y

the devil.

Break a leg

'good luck' when addressed to actors, as to wish them good luck directly would bring the reverse. The phrase is an allusion to bending ('breaking') the knee while taking a bow in front of a rapturous (it is to be hoped!) audience. In France, too, to wish someone good luck does not bring it to them – rather you wish them *merde* (sh*t) – but only in informal exchanges.

Cloot, clootie, old cloot etc.

the devil. A cloot is a division of a cloven hoof (the devil has cloven hoofs instead of feet).

Dark man, dark one, the

the devil, for the darkness of his deeds.

Eumenides, the

'the Kindly Ones'. Three ancient goddesses in Greek legend, usually portrayed with snakes for hair and eyes that dripped blood, like the Gorgons – not kindly sounding! They were later identified with the Erinyes, the Furies, three avenging goddesses who were merciless in their pursuit of wrongdoers in the name of justice.

Euxine

meaning 'the hospitable' – the Greeks gave this name to the dangerous, stormy Black Sea. This is not unlike the renaming of 'the Cape of Storms', except in that case there was more than an element of 'commercial PR' – originally named by the first European to sail round it (the Portuguese navigator Bartolomeu Dias, in 1488), South Africa's southernmost point was shortly after renamed the Cape of Good Hope by Portugal's king, John II, who was not slow to see its potential as a trade route, and considered Dias's name for it off-putting.

Gentle people
fairies, who were seen as malicious little creatures in times past: if you did not speak nicely of them, it was thought they were quite likely to do something nasty to you.

Good folk, good people
fairies.

Good man
the devil, who is even less likely to recognize this as himself.

Grunter
a pig. Pigs and boars were a cult animal among Celts and other ancient tribes of the British Isles – to mention them in the context of, say, pork could invite repercussions.

Hangie
the devil (a corruption of 'horny'?): 'O thou! whatever title suit thee –/Auld Hornie, Satan, Nick, or Clootie!/ … /Hear me, Auld Hangie, for a wee …' – Robert Burns, 'Address to the Devil' (1786).

Harry, old Harry
the devil.

Hornie, old Hornie/Horny
the devil – for he has horns.

Little folk, little people
those malicious fairies again – not a derogatory comment so much as an attempt to suggest that they are attractive.

Mappie
a rabbit. Hares were considered sacred animals by ancient British tribes, and rabbits too by association. They were said to be shape-shifters who could turn themselves into witches.

Nick, old Nick, Nickie, Nicker
the devil – an evil water spirit, from Anglo-Saxon *nicor*, 'marine monster', related to Danish *nikker*, 'water sprite'. Not from the name Nicholas, in spite of the propensity the devil shares with Santa Claus for going down chimneys.

Old bendy/boots/child/gooseberry/serpent/sooty/toast/ whistler
the devil; the thinking behind some of the names is fairly clear, others remain obscure.

Prince of Darkness, the
the devil.

Reid fish
salmon. The salmon was revered as a sacred creature by the Celts – who thought it to be a manifestation of their god Nodon. Fishermen, especially Scottish fishermen, have always been highly superstitious.

Sandy Campbell, Sonny Cammie
a pig, 'Campbell' possibly from the name of the clan responsible for the Glencoe massacre, perhaps linked here to the pig's destined slaughter (see also 'grunter').

Scottish play, the
actors, a superstitious bunch, consider it unlucky to mention Shakespeare's *Macbeth* by name, as to do so will supposedly invite all manner of catastrophe upon the cast.

Scratch, old Scratch
the devil – probably from the Old Norse word *skratte*, meaning a wizard, goblin, monster, or devil. 'Old Scratch has got his own at last, hey?' (Charles Dickens, *A Christmas Carol*).

Smoker
the devil – no hellfire without smoke?

Thief, old thief, black thief, thief of the world
the devil.

Wee folk, wee people
fairies, as in 'little folk'.

Wise man, woman
a feared witch, male or female.

To do with death, dying and killing

Death and dying

Death. It is the great unknown and, whatever a person's religion or beliefs, or however scientific they may be, it raises nameless fears. For many, it is a taboo subject: a hangover from centuries of superstition, grief, fear and determined avoidance of the topic. With death, there is not just the fear of one's own death and the deaths of those one loves, but we also feel grief for the deaths of others; helping friends and family to cope with their own losses can be equally traumatic. Until comparatively recently, the study of death and dying was taboo, and many still consider it insensitive. Most people prefer not to dwell on the subject – to the extent that many cannot bring themselves to discuss it except through euphemism.

It is this combination of fear and avoidance that has given rise to an enormous number of euphemistic terms for death. Interestingly, the majority of these take the form of metaphors that can seem arch, harsh, mocking and insensitive – perhaps they are more accurately termed dysphemisms (for example, 'pushing up the daisies') or, occasionally, cacophemisms ('worm food'). Even a phrase with a most respectable provenance, 'to give up the ghost' (Job 14:10 – 'Man dieth and wasteth away; yea, man giveth up the ghost'), would sound inappropriate in the normal course of events. Surely, assuming conventional  circumstances and emotions, nobody would say, 'My father gave up the ghost last week'? They are much more likely to say, 'My car gave up the ghost this morning.'

The – far from comprehensive – list below shows how a large number of euphemisms relating to death are humorous, or try to be: misplaced frivolity, some will think, but the flippancy is more accurately a kind of defiance, the apparent insensitivity a form of whistling past the graveyard, a refusal to recognize or accept the fact of death, or that it worries you in any way. Thus many of these euphemisms tend to be borrowings from other areas of life – very often from the workplace, for instance suggesting a retirement from hard grind.

Gravestones have their own language, largely euphemistic and often very sentimental. But that is traditional and – on the whole – we accept it for what it is (or what it is meant to be): a reflection of the dead person's family's and friends' grief. On the lips of most people today, however, the sentiments expressed sound false. We are not gravestones. Our language has to be alive, even if that means it appears blunt or harsh.

Abraham's bosom, go to, to be in
    to die, to be dead.
Account, go to one's last
    to die.
Afterlife, to have gone to the, to be in the
    to die, to be dead.
Answer the call, to
    to die, usually at war, having been called to arms.

Arrest

death ('that fell arrest', William Shakespeare, 'Sonnet LXXIV').

Asleep in Jesus, to be

dead (gravestone language).

Assume room temperature

die; an obvious allusion to a corpse cooling down.

At peace/at rest, to be

dead (gravestone language, but, it could be argued, true in some cases – as of those who suffered severe chronic pain – and a comfort to the dead person's friends and family).

Beamed up, to be

to die, an allusion to *Star Trek*.

Better place/country/world, in a

as 'At peace …'.

Big D, the

death.

Big jump, the

death (probably not from 'did he jump – or was he pushed?').

Big stand-easy, the

death (in the military).

Bite it

dysphemism, probably a reference to 'bite the dust'.

Bite the big one

as 'bite it', plus 'the big D'.

Bite the biscuit

as 'bite it' (and tastes better than dust).

Bite the dust

die, usually violently, the implication being that the person falls to the ground; there could also be a reference there to being buried (see 'dirt nap'). Dysphemism rather than euphemism.

Bonds of life, the

'the bonds of life gradually dissolving she winged her flight from this world in expectation of a better' – or, put more simply, 'she died'. The lines come from a stone at Bath Abbey, a splendidly roundabout epitaph, comforting in its evasion of the hard truth and its suggestion of a new and happy freedom (though you are left hoping that 'gradually dissolving' does not mean a painfully slow death).

Box

coffin; as in 'come/go home in a box', which is generally applied to soldiers killed in action on foreign soil.

Breathe your last, to

to die – circumlocution rather than euphemism.

Buy the box/a pine condo

acquire a coffin – i.e. to die.

Buy the farm

an American expression: from the fact that so many US citizens dream of owning a farm after they have retired.

Cache in your chips

a computer nerd's variation of 'cash in your chips'.

Cash in, cash in your chips (and variations)

an expression that probably originates from gambling, where on leaving the table you hand over your chips in exchange for money (if you've been lucky). Many euphemisms for death have a theme of reckoning, financial or otherwise.

Ceased to be among us, has

has died – Patrick Leclercq, Monaco's minister of state, announced the death of Prince Rainier in April 2005 in this carefully circumlocutory manner.

Condition non-conducive to life

facetious circumlocution: terminally ill, about to die.

Croak, croak one's last, to
  dysphemism arising from the sound a dying person, unable to clear his or her throat, sometimes makes.

Cross the bar
  from Alfred, Lord Tennyson's 'Crossing the Bar': 'I hope to see my Pilot face to face/When I have crossed the bar' (1889).

Cross the great divide
  die: the idea of crossing from one world to another is common in metaphors for dying.

Cross the Jordan/the river
  die – variations of 'cross the Styx'.

Cross the Styx
  In Greek mythology, Charon, the ferryman, would take the souls of the dead across the river Styx to the Underworld – as long as they had been buried with a coin in the mouth as payment for the crossing.

Curtains
  the play – life – has ended (as Shakespeare said, 'All the world's a stage', *As You Like It*).

Cut the painter, to
  to die; the allusion is to casting a boat adrift – in this case cutting the bond to life (see 'bonds of life').

Davy Jones's locker
  the 'graveyard' at the bottom of the sea, where those who have drowned or been buried at sea are supposed to go. Davy Jones is the devil, or evil spirit of the ocean.

Dead meat
  dead; a dysphemism if not a cacophemism when uttered as a threat, as in: 'you are dead meat if you snitch'.

Deceased
  the dead person; a convenient dysphemism, as it can refer to the body or be applied as an adjective.

Depart this life
  die (off to a better place?).
Departed, dearly departed
  dead person (e.g. in funeral-speak).
Dirt nap, to have or take
  facetious reference to being dead and buried.

End, end of the line, of the road, to reach the
  to die – but this phrase is ambiguous depending on the
  context, it could equally refer to a stage in one's life –
  marriage, career, etc.
Eternal life
  death.
Eternity, in
  dead; if you are 'launched into eternity' you die or are
  killed.

Fade away
  to die.
Feet first
  dead – traditionally the dead are carried out of rooms feet
  first.
Ferryman
  death personified (e.g. 'that grim ferryman' from William
  Shakespeare, *Richard III*); see also 'cross the Styx'.
Fertilizer business, to go into the
  a dysphemistic reference to being buried.
Final arrangements
  bland funeral-speak to cover the funeral and burial or
  cremation.
Funeral director
  undertaker; in the States 'undertaker' was first replaced by
  'mortician'. Now, it is reported, some like to call themselves

'grief therapists'. (And undertakers were once mere grave diggers …)

Gathered

to be gathered to one's fathers or ancestors/God/Jesus/ Mohammed etc. – as 'Abraham's bosom'; also a good gravestone standby.

Give an obol to Charon

a facetious rendering of 'cross the Styx'; an obol was a small, ancient Greek coin.

Give up the ghost

to die; the ghost is your soul or spirit and you surrender it to God on your death. Job 14:10, 'Man dieth, and wasteth away; yea, man giveth up the ghost.'

Go, to

to die. The dying just 'go' ('she's gone'), or else they go somewhere named but unspecified (e.g. to a better place, a final reward, Heaven, a happy hunting ground, etc.); some go for a 'Burton' (RAF slang from the Second World War, possibly referring to ale from Burton-upon-Trent); but first check the context of this phrase, as it can also mean 'ruined', 'destroyed' or 'fallen flat' – as in career or plans – and it would be dreadful to get the various meanings confused. On their way to 'going places', sometimes the dying also 'cross a river' or a 'great divide'; sometimes they go through a door. To the anxious crowd in St Peter's Square, Rome, in April 2005, Monsignor Camastri, Vicar-General for the Vatican City, said: 'This evening or this night, Christ opens the door to the Pope.'

Goner, to be a

to be dead ('gone').

Great certainty/change/leveller
death; a dead writer might go to the 'great book-signing in the sky', a dead shopaholic might go to 'the great superstore in the sky', etc.

Grim reaper, the
death personified.

Halo, get your
to die and go to heaven – somewhat presumptive, perhaps.

Hand in/hang up your dinner pail/hat/mug/spoon/tack
to die: you're not going to need any of these objects any longer.

Happy hunting ground, to go to the
to die. Said to be where Native Americans go after death.

Happy release
death – usually of one who has suffered long and painfully; rather mealy-mouthed and you might wonder if what is meant is, in fact, a happy release for those who looked after the dying person.

Harp, to pick up your
as 'get your halo'.

Heart … its final pause
as in 'his heart came to its final pause' – a circumlocutory way of saying 'he died'.

Home, to go to one's last
to die.

In God's hands
dead; Cardinal Camillo Ruini, the Vicar of Rome, announced the death of the pontiff on 2 April 2005 by saying that Pope John Paul II had 'completely left himself in God's hands'.

In the arms of ancestors/fathers/Jesus/Mohammed etc.
to be dead.

Join one's ancestors/the angels, to
    to die.

Kick the bucket, to
    to die. Thought to be from slaughtering
    livestock; the animal's legs would kick out in its
    death spasms. The origin of the 'bucket' has
    been lost in time; it might be a kind of beam to
    which a pig was tied ready for slaughter – or it could be a
    bucket standing nearby to collect the blood. There are,
    however, alternative suggestions that the entire expression
    comes from hanging, the premise being that the person
    being hanged or hanging himself stands on a bucket, which
    is then kicked away. (The argument against this is that a
    bucket is not the most obvious object to stand on – a stool,
    box or chair would be more likely.)

Kiss/lick the dust
    to die, with the suggestion of suddenness, as in falling to
    the ground, being killed: 'His enemies shall lick the dust'
    (Psalm 72:9). See also 'bite the dust'.

Kumantjayi
    in Australia, among some Aboriginal cultures, to mention a
    dead person by their first name is taboo – and in such cases
    the person's first name is replaced by 'Kumantjayi'.

Last call, round-up, trump, the
    death.

Last debt, to pay your
    to die.

Last journey/resting-place/voyage
    death.

Lay down your burden/knife and fork, to
    to die – see 'hand in/hang up' above.

Lay down your life, to
> to be killed – often carrying the suggestion that a person has sacrificed his or her own life in order to save someone else's.

Legs, to be on one's last
> dying.

Living-challenged/living-impaired
> dead or dying – satirizing politically correct language.

Lose one's life, to
> to die, often prematurely in some disaster.

Loved one, the
> the dead person/the body. Note: not exclusively used as a euphemism for a deceased friend or family member.

Maker, to go to meet one's
> gravestone language for 'to die'.

Meet the Prophet, to go to
> to die.

Moderator
> death. 'This reasonable moderator, and equal piece of justice, Death' (Sir Thomas Browne, *Religio Medici*).

Move into upper management
> to die, jocular use of business terminology.

Negative patient care outcome
> facetious interpretation of how a politically correct hospital might refer to a patient's death.

Night
> death: 'Do not go gentle into that good night' (Dylan Thomas).

Out of print, permanently out of print
> dead (specific to the book trade).

Oxygen habit, to kick the
> to die; a reference to overcoming an addiction.

Pass, pass away, pass on, pass over, to

to die; 'pass away' is probably the most frequently used euphemism for 'to die' and as such has become, like 'toilet', a widely accepted synonym, although there are those who consider these terms over-genteel.

Pay one's debt, to

many see life as a loan – which is paid back by dying.

Peg out

to die, a reference to the game of cribbage, in which the player who finishes first places his peg in a row of holes on the board.

Pop off

to go – by extension, to die. You have to watch the context: someone might have 'popped off to the corner shop' in which case he's very much alive, or he might have 'popped off', in which case his state of being is in question.

Pop your clogs

a variation of 'hand in your dinner pail'.

Push up the daisies

to be dead – and buried (and part of the nitrogen cycle, thus helping the daisies to grow).

Reaper, the Grim

death personified.

Reformatted by God

dead – a computer-nerd euphemism.

Remaindered

dead; specific to the book trade.

Repose, to

to be dead and buried.

Reposing room

morgue in funeral-speak.

Rest, at

dead.

Rest, to go to one's
to die.

Ring eight bells, to
to die; on board ship, eight bells were rung to mark
the end of one watch and the beginning of the next – an
allusion to the watch (life) being over. There is also the
suggestion of funeral bells tolling.

Sergeant
'this fell sergeant, death' (William Shakespeare, *Hamlet*).

Setter up and plucker down of kings
death (William Shakespeare, *Henry VI, Part III*).

Shuffle off this mortal coil
to die; an intriguing metaphor, perhaps an allusion to the
soul's escape from the mortal body being like a butterfly
freeing itself from the chrysalis. The phrase is from
Shakespeare's *Hamlet*.

Singing with the angels
dead (gravestone language). See also 'harp' and 'halo'.

Six feet under
dead and buried.

Sleep, the big sleep, a little sleep
death (sometimes the euphemism is 'slumber').

Sleeping with the fishes, to be
to be dead; gangster-speak, sometimes used as a threat,
more often in a reference to some unfortunate the gangsters
have put in 'concrete boots' (see Killing section) and cast
into the river … never to be seen alive again.

Snuff it, to
to die (life snuffed out like a candle).

Stiff
dead body.

Street pizza
offensive to those involved in any way, otherwise a colourful

dysphemism for someone killed in a road accident.

Substantive negative outcome

death; doublespeak: this could follow military action.

Sweet hereafter, in the

dead (and in heaven).

Taken

dead – taken from this world to the next.

Taps

death, as in 'It's taps for him'; from 'taps' or tattoo, the drum roll or bugle call that signals the end of a military day; and by association the end of a life: the breath-catching lone bugle call, the 'Last Post', for example, is often sounded at military funerals or memorial services (famously, at the Remembrance Sunday ceremony at the Cenotaph in London).

Toes up

from 'turn up your toes'.

Turn up your toes

to die. Most people die lying in a bed, usually on their back – therefore with their toes pointing upwards.

Turn your face to the wall

to die – turning one's face to the wall in order to die in privacy; it is also seen as a final gesture of acceptance. In the Bible, Hezekiah has been sent a message by the Lord that he will die 'and not live': 'Then he [Hezekiah] turned his face to the wall, and prayed unto the Lord.' (2 Kings 20:2). From 2 Kings 20:21: 'And Hezekiah slept with his fathers' – i.e. died.

Under the grass/daisies/sod

dead and buried.

Undiscovered country, the

'… from whose bourn/No traveller returns': death (from William Shakespeare's *Hamlet*).

Wages of sin
death: Romans 6:23 'For the wages of sin is death'. (For the sinless, 'the gift of God is eternal life through Jesus Christ our Lord' – see 'eternal life', 'eternity').

Way of all flesh, to go the
to die (from Joshua 23:14 in the Douay-Rheims Catholic Bible of 1609, by way of Samuel Butler's classic *The Way of All Flesh*, pub. 1903).

Way of all the earth, to go the
to die; 'I am going the way of all the earth' (Joshua 23:14).

With Jesus, with the Lord
sentimental gravestone language.

Worm food
dead and buried (sometimes as 'food for worms').

Written out of the script
dead (depending on the context, as it can also mean simply dismissed or sacked). A dysphemism from the world of theatre and film.

And now for something completely different … A collection of euphemisms for 'dead', but all in the one outburst – John Cleese's tirade at the pet-shop owner in the 'Dead Parrot' sketch, from *Monty Python's Flying Circus* (BBC). This is just one of the many versions of the speech.

'E's not pinin'. 'E's passed on. This parrot is no more. He has ceased to be. 'E's expired and gone to meet his maker. 'E's a stiff. Bereft of life, 'e rests in peace! If you hadn't nailed 'im to the perch 'e'd be pushing up the daisies. 'Is metabolic processes are now 'istory. 'E's off the twig! 'E's kicked the bucket. 'E's shuffled off this mortal coil, run down the curtain and joined the bleedin' choir *invisibule*! THIS IS AN EX-PARROT!

Killing

Killing, though not taboo in quite the same way that death is (in spite of it being a vehicle of death), has its own generous share of metaphors. From the evasive language of the compassionate human talking about killing pet animals, to the colourful, often brutal dysphemisms of mobsters, through to the deliberately ambiguous language, the doublespeak, of military organizations, the act of killing and its various accoutrements have produced a wealth of euphemisms. And, while governments and military organizations go out of their way to obfuscate references to actual killing, sports commentators – among others – enthusiastically employ 'killing' metaphors: thus a defeated team is 'thrashed', 'destroyed', 'slain' – emotive words to capture attention.

Abattoir
> slaughterhouse; a foreign word seems less harsh to an animal-loving nation ('abattoir' comes from the French *abattre*, 'to fell').

Ace
> (US) to kill; from card playing.

Annihilate
> to kill, but this word does not always deal with death – it is often used in reports of competitive games as a dysphemism for 'defeat conclusively': a peaceful Martian watching Earth TV would be very startled to hear the announcement that 'Ireland annihilated Wales', when the only possible weapon to be seen is a strangely shaped ball.

Anti-choice
> what pro-abortionists call anti-abortionists.

Anti-personnel
> literally 'against people', but used as a euphemism for weapons designed to kill.

Assassination

murder, usually for ideological or political reasons, so to some viewpoints there might be a justification of sorts for the killing. This would of course depend upon one's perspective … The assassin is sometimes a hitman, hired by an individual or even government; at other times assassins act entirely independently.

Auto-da-fé

literally 'act of faith', in fact burning to death (from the time of the Inquisition).

Axe, to

to execute, originally by beheading; now a dysphemism for summary dismissal.

Baby killers

anti-abortionist cacophemism for pro-abortionists.

Bag, to

to kill (as in hunting).

Blot out, to

to kill (with extreme thoroughness implied).

Blow away, to

to kill, usually by shooting at close range.

Bucket, to

to drown (newborn kittens, etc.) – a dysphemism for an animal-loving nation.

Bump off, to

to kill (with the implication of a contract killing).

Burke

murder; after William Burke, who, with William Hare, provided dead bodies to Edinburgh's renowned medical schools in the nineteenth century, initially by robbing graves, then by the more direct means of murder (the medical schools were allowed bodies of executed criminals for dissection, but demand outstripped supply). Hare turned

King's Evidence, and went free but died in penury. Burke was hanged (allegedly in front of a crown chanting 'Burke him! Burke him!') and, fittingly, his body ended up on the dissecting table of Edinburgh University's Medical School.

Burn, to

(US) to kill (originally from executions by electric chair, extended to unauthorized shooting).

Capital

to do with killing; literally 'of the head', it originates from execution by beheading; 'capital punishment' is execution.

Cement shoes

gangster killing: see 'concrete boots'.

Chair, the

not a professorship or chairmanship, but the electric chair, i.e. execution.

Chelsea smile, to be given a

to be killed – when the victim's throat has been cut from ear to ear; from the heyday of London's criminal underworld.

Chew a gun, to

dysphemism for committing suicide by shooting oneself in the head, through the roof of the mouth … leaving little to chance.

Collateral damage

a military term to mean the unintentional killing or injuring of innocent civilian bystanders. The casual tone of the euphemism contrives to make these incidents seem no worse than some light damage to property.

Collect a bullet, to

to be killed (by gunshot).

Concrete boots

US gangster 'execution'; variations include cement/concrete shoes, galoshes, overcoat. The reference is to the body being weighted to ensure it sinks to the bottom of the river (or whatever other body of water it is thrown into).

Contract

in the criminal underworld, an ordered killing ('to put a contract out on someone'); by extension 'a contract' could also mean the intended victim.

Crush

although crushing can kill, this is not usually used literally except in specialized circumstances; it is a dysphemism for 'beat the competition' (e.g. 'Their team won a crushing victory').

Cull, to

to kill in the sense of mass slaughter. This solid agricultural term, related to the word 'collect' and the French word *cueillir*, 'to pick' (as in 'pick flowers'), originally meant to pick out the best from a group. It then came to mean to select a proportion of an animal population for slaughter, in order to maintain the health of the majority, and limit their numbers. With the enforced mass slaughter of livestock during the UK's outbreaks of BSE and foot-and-mouth disease, the word 'cull' was seized upon as a palatable term to describe the mandatory killing.

Cut, to

(US) to kill, possibly from the notion of 'cutting a person out of the picture', rather than having anything to do with knives.

Dance, to

to be killed by hanging – the reference is to the twitching and kicking of the swinging body. Here the word on its own might sound euphemistic – the image, however, is anything but.

Deanimate

to kill: a form of doublespeak, chillingly indifferent.

Demote maximally

to kill one of your colleagues; espionage language. Many spy novels turn on the killing of, or orders to kill, a co-agent.

Destroy, to

of animals, a harsher way of saying 'put to sleep' in the case of pets; otherwise a slightly less emotive synonym for 'slaughter'.

Dispose of, to

to kill; cynical treatment of someone who might be an obstacle to a criminal, dictator or secret agent.

Do away with

to kill.

Do in

to kill, as in 'they did him in', or suicide, as in 'she did herself in'.

Eliminate, to

to kill, often in the sense of a secretly sanctioned (i.e. by a security agency or government) – but illegal – assassination. There is also the phonetic suggestion of 'exterminate'.

Ethnic cleansing

at its worst, 'ethnic cleansing' is nothing less than genocide. From the Serbo-Croatian phrase meaning 'ethnic cleaning', *etnicko ciščenje*, current usage dates back only to the 1990s, when it was used, in the first instance by the Yugoslav press and then by international media, to describe the killing, terrorization, and forcible expulsion of non-Serbs from largely Serbian regions of the former Yugoslavia, in order to extend Serbian boundaries (see also 'ethnic cleansing' in the Politics section).

Euthanasia

the painless killing of someone terminally ill. From the Greek for 'well [i.e. good] death', with an 'eu' prefix as in 'euphemism' (see Introduction for salience). See also 'kevork' and 'mercy death/killing'.

Executive action

assassination – generally authorized by the security services.

Final solution, the

the Nazi *Endlösung*: genocide, specifically what is now known as the Holocaust, in which millions of Jews and others were killed in gas chambers.

Fix, to

to kill, as in 'eliminate' or 'dispose of'.

Friendly fire

a military term for an inadvertent attack on you from your own side, from your allies. It does not necessarily involve killing, but when it does it presents the military with the problem of explaining why killing an ally is 'friendly'. This may account for recent references to it by another euphemism, 'incontinent ordnance'. See also 'blue on blue' in the Warfare section.

Go for tea, to

an IRA phrase for 'to be murdered'; if somebody is said to be 'going for his tea', he is due for execution; if an IRA member does not show up at a meeting, for instance, the others might say that he has gone for his tea (though this may, of course, be literal).

Gruesome Gertie

the electric chair; specifically the one in Louisiana, to which death row inmates gave this name.

Ice, to

to kill; a reference to the drop in body temperature – see also 'assume room temperature' under Death and dying.

Kevork

to aid suicide, but it could be extended to mean 'to kill'; from Dr Jack Kevorkian, the American doctor who, in spite of being convicted of murder, remains an advocate of 'physician-assisted suicide'.

Kick the wind, to

see 'dance'.

Knock off, to

to kill – among other meanings depending on the context.

Knock someone on the head, to

to kill; the phrase is also used in other contexts, for example when finishing a project, relationship or evening out, you might 'knock it on the head' to indicate termination of the evening/relationship/project etc.

Liquidate, to

to kill; it carries the same suggestion of ruthless efficiency as 'eliminate'.

Massacre

also used as a dysphemism in reports, for instance, of competitive games – 'Footie team A massacred Footie team B in last night's friendly' ('friendly'?).

Mercy death/killing

the killing of someone terminally ill, or assumed to be terminally ill. Like 'kevork', it can be interpreted as murder.

Necktie party

not a 'formal attire' party, but a lynching; if you are 'measured for a necktie' you are the unlucky victim.

Neutralize, to

to kill, or to disable.

Nobble

to kill (depending on context).

Old Smokey/Old Sparky
the electric chair.

One-way ride
to be taken on one is to be abducted and driven away to be killed – there is no return journey.

Pasted
to 'get pasted' is to die a violent death.

Pick off, to
to kill, with the implication that the victim has been carefully selected; the killer could, for instance, be a sniper.

Plug, to
to kill by shooting; the bullet being the plug.

Pro-choice
what pro-abortionists call themselves.

Pro-life
what anti-abortionists call themselves, the implication being that anyone who supports abortion must be a murderer.

Pull the plug, to
to kill, or rather, allow to die, a reference to euthanasia; the plug is probably that of the life-support machine: unplugged, it stops doing its job. It could also be a metaphor for the patient: unplugged, he stops operating; and there might also be an allusion to 'pulling the plug' (i.e. in a sink or bath) – whereby life is washed away. The phrase is also used in other contexts.

Put down, to
to kill, generally the humane putting to death of a pet; occasionally used of judicial execution (possibly from the writing down of the death sentence), by extension, killing.

Put out a contract on, to
to hire a hitman to kill someone.

Put out of [their] misery, to
the killing of an animal perceived to be suffering.
Put to sleep, to
to kill a suffering or unwanted domestic pet, in theory
painlessly.

Ride the lightning, to
execution by electric chair.
Run into a bullet, to
to get shot dead, the suggestion being that it was
accidental and, indeed, all the victim's fault.

Sanction
an assassination; espionage language (not applied to
associates, see 'demote maximally').
Servicing a target
US military doublespeak – meaning 'killing'.
Sizzlin' Sally
another cheery name for that most uncheery electric chair.
Smoke, to
to shoot dead (from the smoke of
a just-fired firearm).
Smoke it, to
to commit suicide by putting the barrel of a gun in the
mouth and pulling the trigger.

Take, to
to kill (as in hunting animals).
Take care of, to
to deal with, remove, fix … by killing.
Take electricity, to
(US) death by electric chair.
Terminate, to
to kill – to bring a life to an end.

Terminate with extreme prejudice, to

to kill or assassinate, a term which became popular after the release of the film *Apocalypse Now* (1979), in which the phrase was used to describe the central character's mission. The US military has sought to dissociate itself from the actions in the film, but the phrase is in any case usually ascribed to the CIA, who, it is claimed, use it to refer to an assassination. A *Time* magazine article of August 1969 explains, 'In the shadowy world of the intelligence agent, the phrase "to terminate with prejudice" means to blackball an agent administratively so that he cannot work again as an informer. When the phrase "to terminate with extreme prejudice" is used, it often becomes the cloak-and-dagger code for extermination.' ('Extermination' being of course assassination, or murder.)

Top, to

to kill; in spite of the association with 'head' it does not mean specifically beheading; to 'top oneself' is to commit suicide.

Turn off, to

to kill.

Tyburn

all allusions to Tyburn are references to death by hanging. Tyburn was the name given to the notorious gallows which were located near to where London's Marble Arch now stands; the name Tyburn comes from 'two burns [streams]'.

Waste, to

to kill

Wear a Columbian necktie, to

US gangster/drug trafficker 'execution', involving cutting the throat and pulling the tongue out through the slit. As a deterrent to informers this would be pretty effective.

Wear cement shoes, etc., to
　see 'concrete boots'.

Wet work/job/operation
　assassination or 'sanction'; espionage term, attributed to the
　KGB but also to Mossad and the CIA. 'Wet', it is thought,
　because blood is shed (possibly rather a lot) – not an
　allusion to drowning.

Wipe off, to
　to kill, erase.

Wipe out, to
　to kill, erase totally.

Write off, to
　to kill, eliminate, or – in the case of, say, a badly crashed car
　– to destroy; also a reference to removing an item from an
　inventory, or a product from a stocklist (i.e. in a business
　sense), generally with the implication that the product has
　sold badly and the financial losses must be 'written off'.

Write yourself off, to
　to kill yourself.

Yellow Mama
　Alabama's electric chair, so called after it was entirely
　painted with yellow highway paint.

Zap, to
　to kill, with the suggestion of violence; a neologism used
　extensively in computer games, both arcade games where
　you have to 'zap' hostile blobs, and also realistic war games
　where you 'zap the enemy'. The term is also used, however,
　with reference to changing television channels with the
　remote control (or 'zapper').

To do with the 'naughty bits'

Of all taboo subjects, sex is perhaps the one that has spawned the most euphemisms, dysphemisms and other alternative terms for its various aspects. Many will fight shy of using phrases like 'sexual intercourse' or words like 'copulation', and yet be perfectly at ease employing the coarsest of slang expressions; while others seek refuge in circumlocution and genteelism. As with other subjects, new expressions are being coined all the time, and old ones adapted. By and large, all are essentially similar and understandable – in the way of clichéd images in films: the train entering the tunnel, a jack-hammer, a heaving haystack … The taboo nature of sex means that, inevitably, it will often be associated with profanities and – as with excretion – euphemisms have been found for these, through such devices as taboo deformation and rhyming slang.

The selection which follows – split into four subsections – is of necessity only a small percentage of the existing terms, of which many are slightly distasteful, repetitious and quite boring, especially those that carry with them more than a hint of 'laddishness', or men boasting among themselves. On the subject of sex, especially, many of the so-called euphemisms (perhaps more properly termed dysphemisms) are quite often more distasteful than the proper term – usually because of imagery that is violent or embarrassing. The traditional terms, as well as those phrases which are interesting, amusing and colourful, here take precedence. They are rather loosely divided up (because of the ambiguous crossover of the sections) into four areas: sexual acts, the parts of the body associated with sex, sexual professions, and sexual proclivities.

Sexual acts and appurtenances

Act, the

copulation; appears variously as 'act of love', 'of intercourse', 'of shame', etc.

Actaeon

a cuckolder – although Actaeon was in fact no more than a peeping Tom; in Greek mythology he appears as a hunter (and a grandson of Apollo) who, out with his hounds one day, inadvertently (it is said) comes upon Artemis, with her nymphs, preparing to bathe in a spring. So furious is the goddess at being seen unrobed that she instantly turns Actaeon into a stag, so that he will be unable to speak of her nakedness. The hounds, not recognizing the stag as their master, turn on him and tear him to pieces … not the usual fate of cuckolders, however the wronged husbands might feel! Traditionally, the cuckolded husband is shown with horns or antlers, like a stag's, on his head. In this metaphor, the antlers have been transferred from cuckold  to alleged cuckolder. (Not only was Actaeon not a cuckolder, but Artemis was not married.)

Amorous favours/sport

copulation.

Bed, to

to copulate with.

Bonk, to

to copulate; there is a suggestion of a cheerful lack of seriousness, which makes this more of a euphemism than many other metaphors for having sex.

Boom-boom

sexual intercourse.

Carnal act/knowledge/relations

having to do with the sexual act; often used in spite of the connotations of flesh; legal jargon.

Clean up

to copulate (the origin being from the slang for 'to win' – for instance at the card table).

Come, to

to achieve an orgasm; the term 'come together' means to have sexual intercourse, but does not necessarily mean to have simultaneous orgasms. As a euphemistic phrase it goes back a long way: from the Bible, 'When as his mother Mary was espoused to Joseph, before they came together, she was found with child of the Holy Ghost' (Matthew, 1:18).

Condom

a thin rubber sheath, a contraceptive device; the only reason the word could be considered a euphemism is that it apparently bears no relation to its purpose – unless it derives from the Latin word *condere*, which means 'to store/put away/insert/put into'. The origin of the name, however, is uncertain; perhaps it is *condere*, perhaps it is from the French town of Condom or, some say, from a Dr Condom (also French). Whatever its derivation, it has been in use since at least the eighteenth century – if not as a euphemism, at least as an alternative to '[contraceptive] sheath'.

Conjugal rights

legal jargon, but also used generally to mean copulation with your spouse.

Connubial pleasures

pleasures 'to do with marriage' – i.e. copulation, and, therefore, not necessarily involving marriage at all.

Console, to

to have sex with – e.g. when a person's partner is absent for some length of time. (NB: This is quite an arch euphemism; the word 'console' also has far tamer, and far more altruistic meanings in other contexts.)

Copulation

used here as the 'proper term' for sexual intercourse, even though, like 'excretion' in the next chapter, it is in fact a euphemism, originally meaning 'fasten together'. 'Having sexual intercourse with' is awkward and long-winded; 'f**k', a short and immediately understood word, is still considered by many people to be an offensive profanity. (It seems to have been a profanity since the sixteenth or seventeenth century but before that there is evidence that it was acceptable.) As Richard Hoggart said at the trial of D.H. Lawrence's *Lady Chatterley's Lover* in 1960, 'We have no word in English which is neither a long abstraction or a vague euphemism for this act.'

Defile, to
to 'make filthy' – to copulate with, generally understood to mean that the man is the active party, and acting without the woman's eager participation.

Deflower, to
to copulate with a virgin (*noun*: defloration).

Diddle
baby talk for 'masturbate' (when it doesn't mean 'pee').

Die, to
to have an orgasm. There is a French euphemism for orgasm, *la petite mort*, meaning 'little death'.

Discuss Uganda, to
one of the more imaginative euphemisms for having sex. A woman journalist (it is thought, but some say a secretary, some an African princess – her true identity has been lost in urban legend) is said to have explained her absence from a party, having been spotted upstairs with another guest, with the claim that they were 'discussing Uganda' (this was during the 1970s, when Uganda was very much at the forefront of the news). This is doubtless just one of innumerable similar stories spun by couples who 'disappear' together for a while, but this particular flimsy excuse came to the attention of the satirical magazine *Private Eye*, which made the most of it and has indeed introduced it into the English language.

Disport amorously
frolicking and a bit more … to copulate.

Earth moved for [me], the

to have an orgasm. Usually said of women.

Enjoy/enjoy the favours of

have sex with.

Fornication

the act of sex with someone one is not married to – used formally or humorously.

Freak

anything deemed abnormal or unusual; originally a substitute for the 'F-word', it is used widely, even in children's literature, in spite of its origin. Recently, the word has been employed in some pop songs with its initial, sexual meaning restored.

French letter

contraceptive sheath, condom.

Frenching

kissing using tongues.

Get, to

found in many slang phrases to do with copulation, and initial petting – e.g. 'get it together', 'get off with', 'get a leg over'.

Go all the way/the whole way

to have sex (after preliminary kissing and petting).

Hanky-panky

flirtation, or more explicit sexual 'playing around'.

Have, to

to copulate with.

Have it off, to

to copulate.

Horizontal dancing

sexual intercourse.

House of ill fame/ill repute/pleasure
 brothel.
How's-your-father
 a spot of sex, a rather old-fashioned phrase.

Intercourse
 nowadays usually understood as 'sexual intercourse', rather
 than its primary meaning of 'a serious discussion'.
Intimacy
 close relations, but often with the implication of sexual
 relations.
It
 copulation (understood from the context, e.g. 'let's do it',
 'have you done it yet?').

Jig-a-jig
 also 'jig-jig': copulation; from the movement; almost baby
 talk and also sometimes pidgin English.
Johnnie
 a condom.

Knight of Hornsey
 cuckold, a man whose wife has been unfaithful – a play on
 'horns'.
Know, to
 to copulate with, an old euphemism – see 'come together': a
 few lines on from the quotation given there, Joseph 'knew
 her not till she had brought forth her firstborn son: and he
 called his name Jesus' (Matthew 1:25).
Lay, to
 to have sexual intercourse with; also 'I got laid last night'
 means to have had sexual intercourse the evening before.

Letting your fingers do the walking
female masturbation, from the advertising slogan for the Yellow Pages.

Lie with, to
to copulate with, rather than just lie down with. Now rather archaic.

Lip lock
kiss.

Make love to
this once meant no more than 'flirt with', but has since become a euphemism for 'copulate with'; to 'make love' is now 'to copulate'.

Make sheep's eyes at
to show sexual interest in, but with the implication of foolishness or besottedness, and of the interest not being returned.

Make the beast with two backs
to copulate (in Shakespeare's *Othello*, the scheming Iago arouses the anger of Desdemona's father by telling him, 'Your daughter and the Moor are now making the beast with two backs').

Member for Horncastle
cuckold – see also 'knight of Hornsey'.

National indoor game
sexual intercourse.

Neck, to
to kiss and caress. Rather an old-fashioned term now.

Onanism
masturbation, after the biblical story of Onan, who was slain by the Lord after he 'spilled [his seed] on the ground' (Genesis 38:4–10).

Pill, the
it could be any pill, but when the 'P' is capitalized and the word is preceded by 'the', this nearly always means the contraceptive pill.

Prophylactic
the word literally means 'something to prevent something else' – and in this case is used to mean a contraceptive device, i.e. to prevent conception.

Pudenda
genitals (usually a woman's); literally means 'things to be ashamed of'.

Roll in the hay
to have sexual intercourse … with a cheerful agricultural flavour.

Rosie Palm and her five beautiful daughters
one of the more innocent-sounding euphemisms for male masturbation.

Rubber
a condom, after the material it's made from.

Screw, to
to copulate, from the male action but used of both sexes.

Secret vice
masturbation.

Sex
(noun) male or female; but it is often used to mean 'copulation' – especially now that the word 'gender' is increasingly being used in its original place.

Sex, to have/to do
to copulate.

Sexual intercourse
copulation.

Sleep with, to

the most commonly used euphemistic phrase for 'copulate with'.

Smooch

kiss.

Snog

kiss.

Something for the weekend

circumlocutory – condom, from the time when they were acquired at barbershops; the barber, writing out his bill, might ask solicitously, 'And … something for the weekend, sir?'

Tongue-wrestle

kiss.

Tonsil-hockey/-tennis

kiss.

Tumble, to

to copulate.

Ugandan affairs

see 'discuss Uganda'.

Warm a bed, to

of a woman, to copulate, have an affair (i.e. with the owner of the bed, who is not her husband).

Wrong side of the blanket, born on the

illegitimate.

You-know-what

in the context of sex, copulation; it could also be anything else that might embarrass the speaker.

The 'naughty bits'

Amply endowed
of a woman, having large breasts.

Balls
testicles; for some strange reason also a metaphor for courage (when it can be used of women as well).

Below stairs
genitalia.

Bits
male genitalia.

Bollocks
testicles (possibly from 'balls' via 'ballocks'); also means 'rubbish, nonsense'.

Boobs
breasts; a 'boob' is a silly or embarrassing mistake, but the origin is probably 'booby', slang for a very stupid person.

Bosom
breasts or breast in the sense of 'chest'; very genteel people might, however, refer to a woman's breasts as her 'chest'.

Cobblers
testicles, from the rhyming slang 'cobblers' awls/balls'; like bollocks, it also means 'rubbish, nonsense'.

Cock
already in use in Shakespeare's day, used as slang for 'penis'; it has several other meanings (along with the main one of male bird), among them (again), 'rubbish, nonsense'.

Derrière
a genteelism (because it's a foreign word) for 'bottom' (it is more accurately translated as 'behind' or 'backside'). See

also the section on Everyday genteelisms.

Ding-a-ling

penis (perhaps because it hangs down like a bell clapper).

Dong

an extension of the above (but a 'ding-dong' is a fierce argument, rather than a well-endowed man).

Downstairs

genitalia.

Equipment

male genitalia.

Family jewels

male genitalia, perhaps an allusion to the value of their role in making a family, also to signify their importance and precious nature as seen by the males of the species (sometimes called 'jewels' or 'crown jewels').

Intimate parts

genitalia.

John Thomas

one of the more common names given to the penis.

Knackers

testicles; probably from the dialect word 'knacker' for a kind of castanet (i.e. bits hanging), and nothing to do with being knackered, which is when you are fit for the knacker's yard – where horses and other working animals were sent for slaughter when they were no longer able to work.

Lunch box

male genitalia.

Naughty bits
genitalia.
Nether regions
genitalia.

Pecker
penis.
Pneumatic
of a woman, having large bouncy breasts.
Privates
genitalia; also 'private parts', 'privy parts'.

Short-and-curlies
pubic hair; also 'short hairs'.

Tackle
male genitalia.
Tool
penis; could it be, one wonders, a screwdriver?

Vagina
although now used as the 'proper' term for female genitalia, it is in fact an early euphemism from the Latin (which originally meant 'scabbard, sheath' – so what could the sword be …?).
Vital statistics
a woman's figure – her breasts, waist and hips, the 'statistics' being the measurements thereof.

Well endowed/well hung
having a large penis.
Whatsit
penis.

Willie/willy

   penis; widely accepted euphemism and one commonly used
   with small children.

Marketplace sex

Adult

   (as adjective) sexually oriented – i.e. pornography (which
   word originates from the Greek *pornographos*, meaning
   'writing about prostitutes').

Alley cat

   prostitute (from haunting dark side streets); as a verb it
   means 'behaving promiscuously'.

Blue

   erotic (as in 'blue film'); probably from the French
   Bibliothéque bleue, a collection of erotic writings.

Bodice-ripper

   a novel or film with pornographic scenes.

Courtesan

   a prostitute, but a high-class, expensive one, now of a dying
   breed. Courtesans were said to be more than prostitutes –
   no single sordid nights for them – although they were less
   than mistresses. The word ultimately derives from the word
   'court', the implication being that courtesans' customers
   were courtiers, and others of a similar social standing; the
   courtesan selected her clients carefully and was shown off
   as a status symbol, declaring to the world that the
   gentleman in question could afford to keep an expensive
   woman. She exercised a fair amount of control over her
   own life – but as the money lavished on her was to be spent
   on expensive clothes, it was rare for a courtesan to retire

rich … unless she married her last client.

Currency girl

a prostitute who will only take foreigners as clients, to be paid in their native currency (these girls usually work in non-Western countries, insisting on Westerners for clients, as Western currencies are worth much more than local money).

Dancer, erotic or exotic

a stripper.

Daughter of joy

a prostitute, a term which must owe much to wishful thinking.

Fallen woman

a prostitute or a woman who has 'lost her honour' through engaging in extramarital sexual relations.

Gay girl/lady

former expression for prostitute.

Hooker

prostitute; because they 'hook' or 'catch' their client. Henry Mayhew, a Victorian journalist famous for his book *London Labour and the London Poor* (1851), reported on the city's prostitutes in *London Underworld* (1862), and cites one as saying, 'Some nights we go about and don't hook a soul.'

Laced mutton

a prostitute, one of many such euphemisms. In fact, this is almost a dysphemism, since 'mutton' in this sense is pejorative, given that mutton comes from older sheep, and is tougher than tender lamb – the implication being that the prostitute is not in the first flush of youth herself, she could be 'mutton dressed up as lamb', as the expression goes.

Lady of easy (or no) virtue
a prostitute; nowadays generally used ironically.

Lady of the night
a prostitute, a refined Victorian expression. The phrase stayed in use for several decades, especially in what was called 'polite society', but nowadays tends to be used only ironically.

Loose
promiscuous; a 'loose house' is a brothel.

Lost
of women: prostituting themselves.

Oldest profession
prostitution.

Painted woman
a prostitute (though not in the case of *Mona Lisa*, one imagines).

Scarlet woman
a prostitute, and a woman of dubious moral values.

Sex care provider
a politically correct prostitute.

Street-walker
a prostitute.

Trollop
a prostitute; also 'trull', of which 'trollop' is a variation, originally from the German *Trulle*.

Working girl
a prostitute.

Sexual proclivities

Aesthete
a male homosexual (credited with a greater appreciation of beauty than hoi polloi).

Alternative
in sexuality, different from that considered 'normal'.

Ambidextrous/ambivalent
adjectives to describe someone with both heterosexual and homosexual tastes – i.e. bisexual.

Camp
of a man, extravagantly effeminate (quite exaggeratedly so) – it is an attitude often deliberately assumed, possibly to tease heterosexual society, and has come to mean homosexual.

Closet
metaphorical cupboard in which homosexuals conceal their sexuality; when someone reveals their homosexuality, they are said to 'come out of the closet', often shortened to 'come out' (see also 'out').

Confirmed bachelor
evasion – a homosexual (though also has other contexts).

Do you know Dorothy?/Friend of Dorothy
In the mid-twentieth century, this question was a code used by homosexuals to identify one another. Although there are one or two suggestions that it was originally a reference to the American writer and wit Dorothy Parker, the probable origin of the phrase lies in the 1939 film *The Wizard of Oz*. According to the president of the Gay, Lesbian & Bisexual Veterans of America, the gay community of the time identified with the lost, lovable, eccentric misfits the film is peopled with. Judy Garland, who played Dorothy, the main

role, became a gay icon and gays began to call themselves 'friends of Dorothy', after Garland's character.

Double-gaited

bisexual.

Doubtful sexuality

evasion: if a person's sexuality is 'doubtful' it generally means the person is homosexual.

English disease

foreign phrase to mean male homosexuality; the 'English vice' means to derive sexual pleasure through flogging, etc.

Gay

originally this meant 'female prostitute', but it was then taken into common usage meaning 'happy, merry' – at least until the 1960s, when the word came to be used as a euphemism for 'homosexual', specifically male homosexuals to begin with. It fairly successfully ousted the pejorative term 'queer', which, now that it is used rarely (and despite its original meaning of 'strange'), the homosexual community seems to be rehabilitating.

Herveys

'This world consists of men, women, and Herveys.' Lady Mary Wortley Montagu was referring to the colourful John, Lord Hervey (1696–1743), who was elegant, witty and extravagant: he had two wives, several mistresses and two male lovers.

Homosexual

sexual attraction to those of the same sex, from the Greek *homo* meaning 'same' (pronounced 'hommo'); not to be confused with *homo* meaning 'mankind' from the Latin for 'man' (and pronounced 'home-o'). The shortened form 'homo' is considered pejorative.

King Lear

rhyming slang for 'queer'.

Lesbian

originally this meant an inhabitant of the island of Lesbos, in ancient Greece. The lyric poet Sappho, who lived on the island, wrote of love between women in some of her poems. The term now means a homosexual woman.

Love that dare not speak its name

homosexuality (Lord Alfred Douglas, Oscar Wilde's lover 'Bosie', a minor poet, ended his poem 'Two Loves' with the lines '"… I am true Love, I fill/The hearts of boy and girl with mutual flame."/Then sighing, said the other, "Have thy will,/I am the love that dare not speak its name."').

Never married

'was homosexual' – a polite evasion of the sort to be found in obituaries and dictionaries of biography, where ambiguity is the safest path to take. It is left to readers to make up their own minds as to the reason for the person in question never having married (of course, they might have had dozens of opposite-sex lovers and simply never been able to choose among them).

Out

having come out of the closet (see also 'closet'); as a verb, to come out, to reveal yourself as a homosexual or to make it public that someone else is homosexual.

Peeping Tom

one who gets sexual gratification through watching others engaged in sexual activity, a voyeur; said to be named after the man who secretly watched Lady Godiva ride naked through Coventry (she had ordered all the citizens to stay inside, windows shuttered. Tom the tailor peered through the window … and was instantly struck blind).

Pink
a colour associated with homosexuals (see 'pink pound' in the section on Commerce, industry and estate agents); the pink triangle, the Nazi symbol for homosexuals, has been adopted as an international symbol of gay pride and the gay rights movement.

Princess Margaret
an extremely flamboyant male homosexual.

Queer
homosexual male; this derogatory term is now in the process of rehabilitation – among the gay community. There's nowt, as the old saying goes, so queer as folk.

Sapphism
lesbianism; after the ancient Greek poet Sappho of Lesbos, though there is no reason to suppose that she herself was a lesbian (see also 'lesbian').

Stoke-on-Trent
rhyming slang for 'bent' (i.e. the opposite of 'straight', therefore homosexual).

Voyeur
see 'peeping Tom'.

To do with the 'powder room'

While religious euphemisms generally deal with profanity and avoiding blasphemy, and death euphemisms are more concerned with people's sensibilities, those that have to do with the 'powder room' (i.e. the lavatory, and all those natural functions associated with it) cover both profanity and people's discomfort. However, there is a wide gulf between the fear and sorrow brought about by thoughts of death, and the embarrassment and distaste – even revulsion – that people feel for what are, essentially, normal bodily functions.  Whatever the reasons for this (and the dislike we have of bad smells could be one), public reference to excretion of all kinds (excretion here meaning those acts that are known formally as urination, defecation, and vomiting, but also sweating and 'breaking wind'), and the places where the major forms of excretion take place (i.e. lavatories), arouse anxiety and embarrassment in many people – which in turn has generated a particular type of humour, generally called 'toilet humour', and spawned innumerable colourful metaphors, most but not all euphemistic. Alongside these are the more refined euphemisms and genteelisms, including baby talk, defecation being a recurrent topic with babies. A selection follows, but it is worth noting that (as with most other subjects) variations are being coined all the time, and new turns of phrase are being invented that can for the most part be understood in context only.

Ablutions

lavatory; originally a ceremonial act of washing, in the British army it came to mean the place in which you washed, then, by extension, the lavatory. It is still taken to mean the act of washing, sometimes used in place of 'toilette': both terms genteelisms, often used jocularly. NB: The word 'lavatory' is a euphemism as well: it too derives from the idea of washing – the Latin for 'to wash' is *lavare* – but there is no name for the room in which one urinates and defecates, or, more specifically, the room in which resides the receptacle into which one does these things: all the words are euphemisms, dysphemisms, genteelisms, or some other -isms. 'Lavatory' is generally accepted, alongside 'toilet', as being the 'correct' term.

Accident

involuntary urination or defecation – as in a child that wets or soils its pants.

Ajax

lavatory; a nineteenth-century derivation from 'jakes', wits considering it an amusing pun on the name of a hero of the Trojan war.

Amenities

the useful features of a place – a euphemism for lavatory; might be used in mock-ponderous phrases like 'May I avail myself of the amenities?'

Anti-social noise

a fart.

Aunt

lavatory – both require visiting.

Aztec hop/two-step

diarrhoea; tourists are prone to picking up stomach complaints when abroad.

Bathroom

US for lavatory, which is sometimes reasonable as the lavatory is often in the bathroom. But it has its more ridiculous side in such phrases as, 'Your dog is going to the bathroom on my carpet.'

Bathroom tissue

lavatory paper.

Be excused, to

to be allowed to go to the lavatory.

Be sick, to

to vomit – long-established as an acceptable synonym for 'vomit' (which, in spite of being scientific and accurate, is interestingly enough sometimes seen as a genteelism), although it can be ambiguous (used for example to indicate more general illness, or to describe perversion).

Been

'to the lavatory' is understood (as in, to a child before a journey, 'are you sure you've been?').

BO

body odour – telling someone that they have BO is meant to cause less offence than telling them they smell.

Bog, bog house

dysphemism for lavatory; in the days of the outhouse and poor drainage, the ground round the little shed was indeed boggy.

Bog roll

lavatory paper.

Bottom burp

fart (baby talk).

Boys'/little boys' room

(US) lavatory.

Bucket

receptacle in which to defecate; literally a bucket but by extension also lavatory.

Bumf

lavatory paper, though mainly used to mean unnecessary or useless paperwork or junk mail. From 'bum fodder', the implication being that that is all it is fit for.

Business

defecation (but depends on the context) – as in 'the cat did her business in the litter tray'.

Call of nature

generally this is answered – the need to urinate or defecate.

Can

as 'bucket'; it could well be that this is the original can that had to be carried, in phrases like 'they left him to carry the can' – the makeshift lavatory, no more than a bucket, that some poor soldier had to carry, full, from the trenches.

Carsey

lavatory, from Italian *casa*, house. Variously spelt, for example 'khazi' or 'karsy'.

Chamber

euphemistic contraction of 'chamber-pot', which receptacle was, in times past, kept in the sleeping chamber to save on nocturnal journeys to the outhouse, which could be long and unpleasant.

Chunder

vomit; mainly Australian and NZ. Its origin has rival candidates: rhyming slang from a cartoon character called Chunder Loo (Loo/spew); or from the cry 'Watch under!' on board ships, as bucketfuls of waste were poured into the sea.

Cloakroom

lavatory (though occasionally it is purely a place for the temporary sojourn of coats, hats and scarves).

Close stool

portable lavatory, like a chamber-pot.

Closet

lavatory (see 'water closet'). Not to be confused with the homosexual closet (see Sexual proclivities).

Cock the leg

normally what dogs do, sometimes used by men (accompanied by guffaw), who might also ask where the nearest lamppost or tree is, meaning the lavatory.

Comfort station

American genteelism for lavatory.

Convenience

public lavatory.

Crap

faeces, but more commonly used to refer to rubbish or nonsense. Probably originates from the Middle English word for 'chaff', something discarded as worthless.

Defecate

to poo; a euphemism, but it has become the formally accepted term.

Delhi belly

see 'Aztec hop'.

Demands of nature

as in 'call of nature' but maybe more pressing …

Diddle

urinate (depending on the context – it can also be used to mean 'masturbate').

Disgorge

vomit.

Doo, doo-doos

faeces, usually as 'dog doo(s)'.

Droppings

animal excreta – whether bird or elephant.

Dung

animal excreta, manure.

Dunny

lavatory, usually but not exclusively Australian; probably derives from 'dung'.

Duty

see 'business'.

Earth closet or EC

lavatory, usually an outhouse, in which excreta is buried (to become fertilizer), rather than being flushed away.

Emunctory

to do with farting, an uncommon term.

Evacuate

defecate; medical jargon, with an uncomfortable suggestion of drastic steps having been taken.

Excrete

expel as waste – usually taken to mean defecate.

Faeces

scientifically correct but a genteelism for sh*t; the word 'sh*t', still taboo among some, is considered vulgar slang, yet this might arise from its metaphorical use as a swear word or insult, rather than its origin in the Old English word for diarrhoea, *scitte*.

Find a tree

… to pee against; usually used jocularly.

Finish up some paperwork

circumlocutory euphemism for 'go to the lavatory'.

Flying handicap

diarrhoea, which necessitates racing to the lavatory.

Foul

to defecate where it is unacceptable – dogs foul the pavement; a dysentery patient far from any facility might foul his clothes.

Freshen up

US genteelism – if someone goes off to freshen up it usually means that that person goes off to urinate.

Gents

gentlemen's lavatory, the generally accepted term for a men's public loo.

Girls'/little girls' room

(US) lavatory; generally used jocularly, or when talking to small children.

Glow

see 'sweat'.

Go

either urinate or defecate – 'You should have gone before leaving'; also appears as 'go about your business', 'go for a walk', 'go upstairs' (even if the lavatory is not upstairs), etc.

Go to hit the head

Go to the lavatory; see 'head'.

Go where even the emperor must go on foot

i.e. to the lavatory; jocular genteelism.

Go where even the king goes alone

as above.

Gypsy's kiss

rhyming slang – 'piss'.

Head

sailors' terminology. The ship's lavatory was traditionally at the bow or head of the ship.

Heave, to

to retch or vomit.

House train

usually of animals, meaning that they have been taught not to defecate or urinate in the house.

Jakes

lavatory ('Jake's place').

Jerry

receptacle for urine – e.g. a chamber-pot. Also used in the
First and Second World Wars as a slang term for the
German army.

Jimmy

rhyming slang – Jimmy Riddle/piddle.

John

US version of 'Jakes', now used in Britain too.

Ladies

see 'Gents'; the female version.

Latrine

lavatory; mainly used in the military.

Lavatory

euphemism for the place you go to urinate and defecate,
which has many names, all euphemisms or dysphemisms,
genteelisms or evasions. See 'ablutions'.

Little girls'/little boys' room

twee form of 'Ladies' and 'Gents'.

Loo

a happy euphemism for 'lavatory' which manages to be
neither genteel nor offensive. Probably from the French
l'eau, water, possibly via the much older word 'gardyloo'
from the French shout of '*gardez á l'eau!*' as the chamber-
pot was emptied out of the window. It is also suggested,
however, that it derives from the French euphemism for
lavatory, *le lieu* or *lieu d'aisance*; or that it could be from
'Waterloo', which, apparently, was the rather apt name of a
firm that manufactured iron cisterns in the early twentieth
century. The phrase is not directly connected to the Battle
of Waterloo or indeed the town of that name in what is
now Belgium.

Loo roll

lavatory paper.

Men's room/women's room

public conveniences.

Mess

faeces – usually of a child or animal: the baby messes his nappy, and you have to watch out for dog mess on the pavement.

Modern convenience

lavatory – and preferably not an outhouse.

Montezuma's revenge

the bellyaching tourists again …

Motion discomfort bag

sick bag – as provided on board aircraft for you to throw up in.

Napoleon's revenge

… and they're now in France.

Natural functions

urination, defecation and so on.

Nauseated, nauseous

genteelism for feeling sick.

Night bucket

see 'chamber', a less refined version.

Night soil

early lavatories were cleaned of 'soil' by the nightman.

Number one

baby talk – urinate.

Number two

baby talk – defecate.

Odorously challenged

politically correct way of saying someone smells or is very sweaty.

Outhouse

outdoor lavatory, usually pretty primitive; it is what Dr Seuss refers to as the 'euphemism' in the film *It's Grinch Night!* – its being outdoors leading to the child's various adventures.

Pee

urinate; *faire pipi* is French baby talk for 'urinate', so similarly the English could be baby talk, from the sound made, or from the onomatopoeic 'wee' or 'wee-wee', which is also baby talk, with the 'p' from 'piss' replacing the 'w'.

Perform

urinate or defecate, from 'perform a natural function'; might for instance be used by a doctor requiring a sample of one or the other.

Personal hygiene station

(US) genteelism for lavatory.

Perspire

scientific, and also the longer, foreign-sounding synonym for the blunt Anglo-Saxon 'sweat', therefore a genteelism; also see 'sweat'.

Piddle

baby talk/jocular for 'piss' (see below).

Piss

considered vulgar slang for urinate. Onomatopoeic and the same in French (*pisser*); the King James Bible did not see any reason to avoid the word: '… hath he not sent me to the men that sit upon the wall, that they may eat their own dung, and drink their own piss with you?' (Isaiah 36:12).

Plumbing

lavatory.

Point Percy at the porcelain

urinate (of long-winded men, to describe their action).

Polish the mahogany

sit on a nice wooden loo seat.

Porcelain god

lavatory; in connection with vomiting, from kneeling or bowing down before it.

Pony

from rhyming slang 'pony and trap/crap'; perhaps also the suggestion of dung.

Poo

baby talk for faeces, probably from the smell; not used exclusively when talking to small childen as it is descriptive and an acceptable euphemism.

Post a letter (or in the US mail a letter)

to defecate: a euphemistic phrase used to absent yourself from gathered company, also a reference to dropping an object into a receptacle …

Potty

sometimes used as a euphemism for lavatory, from a child's potty, and also 'chamber-pot' (see 'chamber').

Powder one's nose

euphemistic phrase, now often used jocularly by men too, meaning to go to the lavatory.

Powder room

lavatory, specifically for women.

Privy

lavatory (a private place).

Puke

vomit (probably onomatopoeic).

Raspberry

fart; from rhyming slang: 'raspberry tart'.

Relieve oneself

urinate.

Rest room

lavatory; US genteelism.

Sanctum sanctorum

the lavatory; holy of holies.

See a man about a dog (or horse)

to go to the lavatory; periphrasis, often uttered in a joking manner.

Shake hands with the bishop/best friend/wife's best friend/the unemployed, etc.

urinate (men only; and the last example uttered ruefully).

Smallest room

the lavatory. (Winston Churchill once wrote, in reply to an unwelcome letter, 'Dear Sir, I am in the smallest room of the house and your letter is before me. Very soon it will be behind me.')

Soil

human faeces, from 'night soil'. Also used in the same context as 'foul'.

Spanish tummy

those tourists don't give up.

Spend a penny

a long-established acceptable term for urinating, from the time women had to pay a penny to operate British public loos.

Sweat

moisture given off by the body through the pores. It used to be said that 'horses sweat, men perspire, women merely glow'.

Taken short

have an accident (see 'accident' and 'foul'.)

Technicolour yawn

a colourful term for vomit.

Telephone, on the big white phone
being sick into the toilet.

Throne, the
the lavatory.

Throw up, to
a well-established and acceptable, if graphic, euphemism for 'vomit'.

Tinkle
onomatopoeic euphemism for urinate.

Toilet
well-established and much-used euphemism for that place where you urinate and defecate, that is apparently known only by metaphors.

Toilet roll/tissue
genteel term for loo paper.

Training Thomas on the terracotta
periphrasis, see 'point Percy at the porcelain'.

Trouser cough
fart.

Urinate
not a euphemism but although it is the 'correct' term (for 'pee'), it sounds like a genteelism.

Use the facilities/plumbing
ponderous periphrasis for 'go to the lavatory'.

Visit Uncle Charley
periphrasis; to go to the loo.

Visiting card
turd or puddle of pee left by an animal.

WC
water closet – the lavatory; also used in French where it is *les vécés*.

Wash one's hands, to
to use the lavatory genteelly.

Washroom
lavatory.

Water closet
see 'WC'.

Whatyoumaycallit, Whatsit, etc.
lavatory.

White telephone
see 'telephone'; most lavatories are white.

Women's
politically correct ladies' lavatory (see 'Ladies').

You-know-what
lavatory.

To do with commerce, industry and estate agents

The worlds of commerce, business, industry and marketing, from top executives to the grass roots, each have their own language, generally well sprinkled with euphemisms and other metaphors. Arcane language serves to give an air of elitism to the business or organization concerned; it serves, too, as a secret vocabulary among the hierarchy. Some industry language attempts (in the case of 'politically correct' job titles, for instance) to encourage employees or potential employees who might otherwise feel dissatisfied with their jobs, or indeed avoid applying for them. In the case of businesses such as estate agencies, the aim of their language is to make their wares as attractive as possible to potential buyers ... while not actually lying. What follows is but a select collection of euphemisms from various industries and trades – with more than a hint of the new PC (politically correct) consciousness included.

Above your ceiling

above the level of your capabilities (as perceived by others) – a roundabout way of suggesting that demotion might be on the way.

Actor

now replaces 'actress' for women as being more politically correct. While 'poetess' does not sound serious and 'poet' should be used for all poets, male and female, there does not seem to be much reason for dropping 'actress' other than a deliberate avoidance of distinguishing between the sexes (why?). See also 'firefighter'.

Administrative leave

suspended (generally US, and for alleged malpractice).

Agent

a woolly term applied to all manner of employment, generally a person who provides a service, typically one who organizes transactions between two other parties.

Belly up

bankrupt – colourful, a dysphemism rather than a euphemism, but in sounding frivolous it makes the fact of bankruptcy seem less serious. (This has a parallel in the use of flippant terms for 'dead' and 'death'.)

Between jobs

without a job (the euphemism lies in the implicit optimism).

Bijou

tiny (estate agents' euphemism for poky properties).

Blockbuster

jargon to mean a book or film that the publisher or producer hopes will rake in millions.

Bump

sudden dismissal from employment, mostly US, as in 'He got the bump'. Not to be confused with 'bump off' –

see Killing section.

Burton, go for a

to go into liquidation, become bankrupt (of a company); but watch the context.

Cards, your

to be given these means to be sacked.

Carey Street, in

to be bankrupt, from the location (since the 1840s) of the bankruptcy court, in the Thomas More building. There is some debate as to whether this is also the origin of the phrase which now carries the same meaning, 'in Queer Street'; it should be kept in mind, however, that the latter phrase existed before the 1840s – except it seemed not to be specifically about finances, but simply to mean that things in general were not going one's way.

Carpetbagger

an opportunistic and unscrupulous speculator; originally from an American banker who made off with the bank's reserves in a carpet bag.

Cashflow problems

cash flows in and flows out – when more flows out than in, it is a problem – or, in other words, it means, for a company, insolvency; for an individual, it means he or she has run out of money.

Catch a cold, to

to make a loss (not to be confused with other meanings of the phrase, such as contracting the illness of the common cold).

Chairperson

politically correct version of chairman – though the latter has been used for women as well as men. Sometimes the term 'chair', *tout court*, is used – thereby reducing a human being (we hope!) to no more than an inanimate object that is sat upon.

Chapter Eleven, file or go

a US phrase meaning 'to go bankrupt', from Chapter Eleven of the American Bankruptcy Reform Act.

Cherry-pick

a practice of fraudulent stockbrokers, whereby they trade on accounts in the morning, then later pick out the profitable ones for their customer.

Chop, the

prompt dismissal.

Close protection officer

important-sounding job title for a bodyguard.

Compact

estate-agentese for uncomfortably small, with low ceilings.

Complimentary

applied to something you get free of charge, often because that which you asked for originally is either not forthcoming or is substandard – a ploy to deflect complaints.

Convenient

of gardens, estate-agentese for 'very small'; of location, 'convenient for shopping' means right on the noisy, traffic-laden high street; 'convenient for the North' means right next to the north-bound motorway, etc.

Corporate entertainment/hospitality

bribery, or at the very least, buttering-up.

Cosy

estate agents' term for 'compact' (see above), and cluttered.

Cottage

in estate-agentese this is a very small and often inconvenient house.

Counselling

a business euphemism for ticking off an employee.

Custodian

gaining popularity in the US as a substitute for the term 'janitor', itself a euphemism for 'caretaker'.

Daisy chain

in the US, a group of investors who collaborate to inflate the price of a quoted security.

Deceptively spacious

roomier than it looks, according to estate agents.

Dehire

(US) dismiss from employment.

Des. Res.

estate agents' advertising shorthand for 'desirable residence'; see 'residence'.

Development consultant

fundraiser.

Door supervisor

bouncer.

Dose of P45 medicine

a circumlocutory way of saying 'dismissal'; in Britain a person must be given a P45 tax form on leaving employment.

Down the tube

fail, of a business for example, e.g. 'the company's gone down the tube'.

Downsize, to

to dismiss employees (thus reducing the size of the company).

Dutch auction

an auction in which the price is dropped until someone makes a bid.

Easily managed

estate agents' euphemism for 'small'.

Economically inactive
unemployed.

Exclusive
estate-agentese for 'expensive'.

Executive assistant
personal assistant, itself a grander-sounding term for secretary.

Extensively restored
estate-agentese either for expensive or for inappropriately decorated.

Extermination engineer
(US) pest controller, but more important-sounding – see also 'rodent operator'.

Family accommodation
of a house, large, unmanageable and draughty.

Fat cats
business bosses ('top executives'), generally those who award themselves huge salaries and bonuses at the expense of customers and shareholders.

Financial assistance
a loan or grant

Fired, to be
to be dismissed from employment. The dysphemism is a play on the word 'discharge', which is another term for 'dismiss' (from employment): you discharge an employee or you can discharge a gun. Discharging a gun is firing a gun – and so the euphemism came to be.

Firefighter
fireman; there is a strong argument for dropping 'fireman' from use and replacing it with 'firefighter', as the word 'firewoman' is not used, although there are women 'firemen'.

Flight attendant
a reasonable replacement for '[air] steward or stewardess',

which replaced 'air hostess', a word now associated with empty-headedness, and with flirty connotations.

Fudge, to

to make deliberately wrong entries in the accounts.

Garden flat

estate-agentese for a basement flat – often dark and maybe damp.

Ghost

a fictitious employee, whose salary in fact doubles (or triples or more) that of another employee. For example, in countries where corruption is rife, there are companies – even governments – that have on the payroll the names of former employees or of dead people, or invented names, to whom a salary is paid; the money might then go to one or a group of other employees.

Give time to other commitments

a euphemistic phrase for dismissal from employment, face-saving for the employee.

Glass ceiling

an invisible upper limit on the promotional ladder, above which only some people can rise; abilities do not necessarily come into the equation. Whom you know and your sex, however, often do: if you are from a wealthy family or you're a friend of the boss, perhaps even from the same school or university as him, you stand a good chance of breaching this invisible barrier. If you are just a clever, hardworking employee – worse still, a woman (for women do things like have babies or 'female complaints', which might jeopardize their ambitions, and commitment to the company) – then there's not much hope for you. Neither can you cite the 'glass ceiling' and its associated discriminations as a reason for leaving your present company when applying for a job at a similar company;

your personal ambitions will be viewed with some suspicion. Feminists talk of their aim of 'breaking through the glass ceiling', whereby women will be able to secure the senior positions they are currently thwarted in achieving.

Go south, to

to lose value, profits – from the downwards direction of the line on the accountant's profit-and-loss graph, which mirrors that of the compass point.

Golden goodbye/handshake etc.

a large payment or handout to avoid damages when an employee is dismissed early or for no good reason; when the 'golden' prefix is applied to 'hello', the payment is an inducement to join a company; when applied to 'handcuffs', an inducement to stay with the company: all are accepted and acceptable forms of bribery.

Gravy train

substantial extra money for little or no extra effort.

Haircut

major financial loss.

Headcount adjustment

adjusting (i.e. reducing) the number of employees – in other words, a mass dismissal.

Headhunter

a recruiting agent, but with the implication that this is a very important recruiting agent – a kingmaker no less – who only seeks out top executives.

Historic

estate agent's description – it means the house is old.

Home

more than just a house or flat, estate agents would like you to know the building is, in fact, just the place for you.

Human resources

to do with personnel, employees, staff. Applied as a department name as well as a job title/career.

Ideal for modernization

a property in need of much work to make this potential 'home' habitable.

Ideal renovation opportunity

as above, the implication in both phrases being that you are so lucky to be given this opportunity …

Immaculate

an estate agent's interpretation of 'in reasonable decorative order'; this could mean newly and well painted – but in some hideous colour.

Involuntarily leisured

a suggested politically correct term for 'unemployed'.

Irregularities

vague enough to be an evasion of 'corporate accounting fraud'.

Job flexibility

a euphemism for lack of job security.

Job seekers

a euphemism for the unemployed.

Knight of the Golden Fleece

'knight' is a euphemism for an individual associated with any illegal or despised occupation; that of the Golden Fleece is a lawyer (it is not clear if there is an intended pun in the word 'fleece' or whether it refers solely to the wig worn in court).

Landscaped

when the estate agent has made sure the garden has been tidied up.

Lay-offs

originally this was in theory a temporary state of not being needed by the company you worked for, you would resume work there when the sun shone or the ship came in – but it has come to mean mass dismissals.

Liberate, to

to dismiss from employment.

Liquidity crisis

when an individual or company is bankrupt but would rather not recognize the fact.

Lose your shirt, to

to be ruined, or well-nigh ruined, financially.

Made redundant, to be

to be dismissed (can also be 'declared redundant'). In Canada a person who is fired or dismissed is 'made surplus'.

Maintenance person

caretaker.

Materials Reclamation Officer

scrap dealer.

Mixologist

in the US some bartenders find this a preferable title.

Moonlight flit

depart clandestinely, leaving behind unpaid debts.

Moonlighting

working at a second job, or working while drawing unemployment benefit, usually without the knowledge of one's main employers or the taxman.

Negative cash

debt (but with the implicit hope that it is the word 'cash' that is taken on board).

Negative contribution

a loss (see 'negative cash'). This is of course a ridiculous

concept, as a contribution by its very nature cannot
be negative.

Negative employment
unemployment.

Negative equity
when you owe hundreds on a computer that is no longer
state-of-the-art, or on a sofa-bed that has been bounced on
once too often, for instance.

Negative growth
a decline. Growth, like a contribution (see above), cannot
be negative, so there is no literal sense to this phrase or
really to any of the 'negative' phrases above; the impression
people are intended to get is that there is growth, equity
and so on ... it just happens to be negative at the moment.

Negotiable
'we are willing to drop our price if you persevere.'

Never-never, on the
bought on a hire-purchase contract (if you *never* buy
something for which you cannot pay on the spot, you will
never be in debt); see also 'negative equity'.

NIH
'not invented here', therefore assumed to be no good; an
excuse given by companies for not having adopted foreign
ideas or inventions.

Old-fashioned
estate-agentese for 'unmodernized'.

On health grounds, to retire/resign on
euphemistic circumlocution, along the lines of 'give time to
other commitments', to avoid saying you've lost your job.

Oozing with charm and character
a house so described by an estate agent will be badly in
need of repair, redecoration and modernization.

Paper hanger

a person who passes fraudulent cheques or securities.

Peaceful

of a property for sale, a euphemism for 'isolated'.

Period

as 'old-fashioned'; different meanings in different contexts.

Personal assistant

a secretary.

Petroleum transfer technician

US aggrandizement of 'gas-station attendant' (petrol-pump attendant); presumably the use of the English 'petroleum' as opposed to 'gas' makes the job sound that much more exotic.

Phoenix

of a company, one that emerges following a liquidation, with the same proprietors and assets, but a different name – thus possibly avoiding paying debts and other liabilities.

Pied-à-terre

estate agent speak for a very small town flat.

Ping-pong

to pass a rich client from specialist to specialist.

Pink pound

the pound in the pockets of homosexuals, who often earn good incomes and have greater spending power than heterosexuals, who might well have spouses and children to support.

Plant

factory (without the connotations of chimneys belching black smoke, though they may be all too present).

Poison pill

liabilities deliberately accumulated by a company in order to deter unwanted takeover bids.

Police officer

could be a PC PC … again, a reasonable substitute for

'policeman' and the unwieldy 'policewoman' –
as well as sounding more important.

Prairie-dogging

an amusing American phrase to describe the
behaviour of annoying people who keep
standing up to check on other employees in an
open-plan office; prairie dogs, a species of ground squirrel,
are continually popping up out of their holes to survey the
area.

Prestigious

in an estate agent's description this means expensive.

Properties

the houses or flats on an estate agent's list.

Pursue other interests

or, in other words, 'give time to other commitments'.

Rainmaker

one who attracts (a shower of) clients for his company.

Realign

of a company, a euphemism meaning to dismiss a number
of employees (see also 'downsize'); of currency, to devalue it.

Redundant

originally used to mean 'superfluous', 'no longer needed'; to
be made or declared redundant means to be dismissed from
employment. The implication, however, is that it is because
of the 'realignment' of the company (see above) and not
through any fault of the employee(s) concerned.

Refuse collector

a more dignified-sounding title for a dustman.

Residence

estate-agentese for house or flat.

Reutilization marketing yard

junkyard.

RIF or 'Riff' (reduction in force)
an American phrase meaning summary dismissal from employment.

Rightsize
a euphemism for 'downsize', itself a euphemism.

Rodent operator
a euphemism for 'rat catcher', a job which is often known as 'pest controller' – in fact a more accurate term as the work usually deals with other vermin too, e.g. cockroaches.

Rubber cheque
a cheque that will 'bounce', i.e. not clear, because there are insufficient funds to fulfil it.

Sacked, to be
to be dismissed from employment. The phrase is also used as 'to be given the sack'. The 'sack' was originally the bag in which a workman kept his own tools, which he left in the employer's office. When departing the company, the workman would be 'given (back) the sack' of tools.

Sanitation engineer/worker
(US) garbage collector, dustman.

Select
in estate-agentese, 'reasonable' (see also 'prestigious').

Services no longer required
dismissed – but, as with being made redundant, the blow is softened by the implication that the job no longer exists, and the dismissal is therefore not linked to the quality of employee performance.

Sharpen your pencil
ask less or be ready to offer more, to alter one's bargaining stance. A bidder who failed to secure a rail-operating franchise when British Rail was privatized in the 1990s explained that he was disappointed, 'But I did not want to sharpen my pencil as hard as some of the others have done.'

Shoot the moon

to do a 'moonlight flit'.

Shortism

the greedy pursuit of short-term gains – not discrimination against those who are 'vertically challenged'.

Shrinkage

retailers' term for shoplifting, or what is lost through shoplifting.

Site engineer

a caretaker.

Snug

of a property – small, cramped.

Sought-after

'expensive because everyone wants it', hopes the estate agent.

Spanish practices

regular fraudulent behaviour on the part of employees – e.g. falsification of expenses, time sheets, etc. A term which might not find favour in Spain.

Spend more time with one's family

a reason given for quitting your job (or for being dismissed); see also 'pursue other interests', etc.

Stand down, to

to be dismissed, or resign; the suggestion here is that it is a noble gesture on the outgoing employee's part – perhaps to save the company money or face, or to give a promising young colleague a chance. Company executives frequently 'stand down' after humiliating media reports and/or disappointing sales/accounts.

Starter home

a small residence – probably not a 'des. res.' as it would have to be relatively cheap for first-time buyers.

Step down

see 'stand down'.

Street-scene officer

road maintenance worker.

Street-scene enforcement

road maintenance. In a world where traffic-controlling measures such as road humps are known as 'traffic calming', 'enforcement' sounds startlingly aggressive.

Sweet equity

a form of insider dealing – shares issued at below their value to favoured investors.

Technical adjustment/correction

a sudden fall in stockmarket prices; nothing to worry about, they would have you believe – do worry.

Turkey farmer

(US) an unsuccessful businessman.

Uninstalled

dismissed (the phrase originates with a computer-firm executive, who seems to have retained his sense of humour even while losing his job).

Up-and-coming

estate agents' term for a less-than-salubrious district into which they hope to move young professionals.

Upstairs

the senior staff.

Urban renewal

cleaning-up of rough, neglected areas – see 'up-and-coming'.

Used

second-hand; employed especially with cars, in an attempt to suggest that the car is practically as good as new, someone's just had a few 'goes' with it before you.

Visiting fireman
   someone sent by headquarters to check
   on a subsidiary branch.

What the traffic will bear
   a phrase to justify the fees charged or price
   asked.

Written out of the script
   dismissed (as in serialized television dramas where
   an actor, for whatever reason, is no longer wanted
   on the set). Can also mean 'dead' in some
   contexts – so watch your usage!

Yellow-page
   adjective to describe businesses that are considered
   ordinary, even inferior – the exclusive, high-quality ones
   not needing to advertise themselves in the nationally
   comprehensive Yellow Pages directory.

To do with politics, espionage and warfare

Politics and warfare are full of policies and actions that, in their unadulterated form, may be regarded with some suspicion or even horror by the ordinary citizen. Such strategies and activities therefore need to be made palatable to the man – sorry, person – in the street. This is where language is brought into full force, as the powers-that-be manipulate their words in order to neutralize and sanitize what they have to tell the public. Both governments and military organizations use propaganda and doublespeak to mollify the citizens upon whose votes and taxes they rely.

While these bureaucracies bend over backwards to appear open and honest, the organizations responsible for the security of the nation are anxious not to appear foolish by giving anything at all away; and so they have developed their own language, which – given the nature of some of their work – also includes a fair amount of euphemism ...

Absorption

military conquest.

Abuse

torture, in spite of Donald Rumsfeld's assertion that '…
abuse, which I believe technically is different from torture'.

Advisers

troops sent to assist the government of another country in
fighting rebels; representatives of a global power sent to
'advise' a weaker nation. 'Advise' is a useful euphemism,
covering all manner of action.

Aerial ordnance

bombs and missiles.

Agent

in espionage a 'secret agent' – a spy.

Anti-personnel

not 'anti-people' – kills people.

Appeasement

giving in to aggression, or negotiating an agreement.

Area denial munitions

meaningless phrase (how can weapons 'deny' land?), gloss
for 'landmines'.

Asset

a spy, usually a foreign one recruited for the other side.

Baby-sit

to secretly monitor telephone calls.

Back door, through the

passing on information through the wrong or improper
channels.

Bamboo curtain

China's equivalent of the Iron Curtain, describing that
country's restricted contact with foreign states ('iron
curtain' was a phrase adopted and made famous by
Winston Churchill during the Second World War, then used

during the Cold War to refer to the closed societies of the Soviet communist bloc).

Black bag

to do with an illicit inquiry.

Blow the whistle on, to

to reveal confidential, possibly damaging, information.

Blue on blue

see also 'friendly fire' – both the US and the British military tend to use 'blue on blue' for such incidents, whereby an ally inadvertently attacks their own side; from the days when, in military exercises, a 'friendly' side would be designated 'Blue', and the opposing side 'Red'.

Canary trap

a trap to catch an informer or passer-on of secret documents.

Charlie

a substitute name for any subject under discussion (usually one which is taboo); in the case of the secret service it might mean the enemy; a group of troublemakers, on remarking the approach of a policeman, might exclaim, 'Here comes Charlie'. Also used as a euphemism for cocaine.

Classified

secret; in the Second World War confidential information was classified according to how it affected national security.

Clean, to

to kill or evict people of a different (and to the perpetrators therefore unacceptable) race or religion; see also 'ethnic cleansing'.

Cleanse, to

to free from enemy occupation.

Collateral damage

unintentional killing of civilians, also damage, structural or environmental, caused by military operations.

Conflict

war (but it sounds more like 'just a little disagreement').

Counter-attack

an unprovoked attack made to sound like a defensive operation.

Criminal extremist organization

any group perceived to pose a threat; a subjective phrase used to imply that any attack upon this group would be justified.

Crusade

an organized campaign or military attack – with the implication that 'right' is on the side of those mounting the crusade; this was an unhappy choice of word in the case of the current so-called 'war on terror', aimed as it is largely at Muslim nations: for the United States history does not come into it – the term 'crusade' is just a useful and emotive word, combining elements of euphemism and propaganda; for Muslim nations, on the other hand, it brings immediately to mind the series of medieval wars waged by Europeans against Muslims in the name of Christianity (the word 'crusade' coming from the Latin *crux*, 'cross'), though possession of land also played a large part.

Decontaminate

to destroy evidence.

Defence

after the Second World War, in Britain, the War Office, the Ministry of Air and the Admiralty combined to form the Ministry of Defence, avoiding direct connotations of war and aggression; in the States, similarly, the Departments of War and the Navy became the Department of Defense in the 1940s. Germany already had their Department of Defence, which was established before the war began.

Detain
to keep in official custody – i.e. imprison.

Detainee
prisoner of war, often held without formal charge, or recognition of the Geneva Convention (which states that prisoners of war are not criminals, and should be treated humanely and released at the end of hostilities. Calling such prisoners 'detainees' denies them that protection).

Device
any object that is possibly controversial; in this case usually something explosive.

Doctor, to
to adjust.

Dry clean
to check out, for security reasons.

Economical with the truth
the omission of certain important facts so as to convey a version of events that might differ somewhat from the actual truth; lying without actually lying. Governments do it.

Embedding
a recent US military policy of inviting journalists to war, 'embedding' them in advancing military units, sometimes even giving them military dress to intensify the reporters' sense of belonging. It is said that embedded journalists are psychologically inclined to see themselves as part of the military operation – and to word their reports accordingly.

Enemy combatant
prisoner of war, but not according to the Geneva Convention (see also 'detainee').

Ethnic cleansing
genocide; from the killing, terrorization, and forcible expulsion of non-Serbs during the civil war in former Yugoslavia: the Serb government's official attempt to

'establish new borders' during the 1990s. A reported statement by the Serb government, referring to Bosnia and Herzegovina, stated that: 'The region is undergoing ethnic cleansing.' In 1981 the Serbian media claimed that the Albanian administration of Kosovo was creating an 'ethnically clean' territory – this was followed by a purging of Albanians from positions of power (in a state where 90 per cent of the population was Albanian). Similar phrases are known to have been used in Yugoslavia during the Second World War, then generally applied to the enemy; an early usage dates back to May 1941, when the Croatian fascist commander Viktor Guti announced: 'Every Croat who today solicits for our enemies [is] an opponent and disrupter of the prearranged, well-calculated plan for cleansing our Croatia of unwanted elements.' See also 'ethnic cleansing' in the Killing section.

Executive action/measure

political murder, authorized by the security services; it was a term used by the Nazi government during the Second World War.

Extraordinary rendition

the delivery of terror suspects to foreign intelligence services, without official extradition proceedings.

Fifth column

a group of traitors within a country that is working for that country's enemies. The term originates from the Spanish Civil War of 1936–9, when General Mola, leading four columns of troops towards Madrid, declared that he had a fifth column inside the city.

Firm, the

a shady or bogus organization, one that is a front for other, perhaps less legitimate activities.

Frank
blunt adjective to describe exchanges between political leaders which are neither friendly nor fruitful.

Free speech zone
an area set aside for protesters, where they will be allowed by law enforcers to have their say undisturbed, as long as they stay within the marked zone; frequently this is positioned well out of the earshot of any potential supporters protesters might have persuaded to their cause.

Freedom fighter
a terrorist a government sides with.

Friendly fire
inadvertent attack from your own side or from your allies. With friends like these, you might say, who needs enemies? Perhaps friends should be more careful not to kill each other.

Grey suits
people described as 'grey' are those thought to be lacking in personality; 'grey suits' might describe deferential politicians.

Guerrilla
could be a freedom fighter, could be a terrorist: hedge your bets.

Helping police with their inquiries
in truth, this is being questioned by the police regarding an incident (and, it is implied, the interviewee is thought to have had something to do with the crime).

Human intelligence (HUMINT)
information from human sources, such as spies and interrogated prisoners.

Human trafficking
slavery.

Improvised explosive device

bombs used in roadside ambushes on vehicles; possibly described as 'improvised' to reduce their (metaphorical) impact.

Incontinent ordnance

bombs which miss their targets and hit civilians.

Independent security contractor

a mercenary.

Infinite justice

revenge.

Insurgents

those who resist military occupation (properly, rebels or revolutionaries).

Intelligence (INTEL)

information and also sources of information (e.g. spies); 'intelligence' is usually secret, or 'classified'.

Interrogation techniques/methods

these include torture; 'interrogation with prejudice' was a KGB term.

Intervention

invasion.

Involuntary conversion

a plane crash (the aircraft is 'converted' to scrap metal).

Liberate

invade.

Liquidation

unlawful killing, but possibly with the tacit support of authority.

Living space

from the German *Lebensraum*; conquered territory.

Martyr

suicide bomber, as viewed by supporters.

Mole
spy within an organization.

Neutralize
to kill or 'render ineffective' (for example, by imprisonment, distraction or damaging the reputation of).

No comment
Winston Churchill told reporters, 'I think "No comment" is a splendid expression. I am using it again and again', having heard it used by the diplomat Sumner Welles, who was US Undersecretary of State in 1937–42. The phrase is now a stock response of politicians and businessmen to reporters, and eliminates any chance of their being misinterpreted or incriminated by any informative or throwaway statement they might make instead.

Non-core promise
a phrase invented by John Howard, the Australian Prime Minister, to mean a promise not kept – in fact one that from the moment it was made was probably never going to be honoured.

Non-lethal weapons
weapons that are only rarely lethal, so that's alright then.

Normalization
the suppression of rebellion.

NYR
'not yet returned' – Second World War acronym for airmen lost in action.

Occupant
member of an invading force.

Open up
US military for 'to shoot at with every weapon available'.

Peace offensive

the word 'offensive' rather gives the game away: an attack which attempts to gain peace for the aggressor. Peace, once the word is bandied about, becomes nothing more than a prelude to war.

Peacekeeper

member of an occupying force. Also, the American nuclear-warhead-carrying missile, Missile X, or MX, developed in the 1980s, was known as Peacekeeper.

Physical persuasion/pressure

torture.

Post-traumatic stress disorder (PTSD)

the graphic term 'shell shock' from the First World War – an accurate and powerful phrase that makes a direct connection with the horrors of battle – became in the Second World War 'combat fatigue' (originally an American usage), which in turn came to be called by the more neutral term 'operational exhaustion', until, following the Vietnam War, it became 'post-traumatic stress disorder'. This is a typical modern military euphemism in that it makes no reference to battle or warfare at all. At least this means that the term can also be applied to civilians or people from civilian services (such as police, ambulance staff and firefighters) who are suffering from this condition of mental and emotional stress brought about by severe psychological shock, sometimes accompanied by physical injury.

Pre-dawn vertical insertion

early-morning parachute drop of troops and equipment.

Pre-emptive strike

an unprovoked attack (the implication given being that it is in order to prevent an attack, 'attack before you're attacked').

Pre-emptive war

an invasion of a country suspected of preparing to attack your country.

Pre-hostility
build-up of war-making apparatus
before hostilities are initiated.

Protective custody
imprisonment of a person suspected of planning to commit
a crime, or of being a terrorist, without due process of the
law – the implication being that this incarceration is for the
prisoner's own protection, for their own good.

Regime change
euphemistic term for the overthrow of a government.

Relocation
the forcible transportation of people from one place to
another – often with the ultimate purpose of killing them.

Rendition
the deportation of prisoners from one country to another, a
process that does not allow international laws to hinder it;
generally effected for the purpose of torture.

Rogue nation
usually one not aligned with a group of other nations (who
are in agreement regarding the conduct of warfare).

RTU
British Army term – 'returned to unit' – meaning failed, in,
for instance, a qualification course.

Safe house
a refuge – e.g. where foreign spies are taken if they, or the
intelligence they bear, are perceived to be in danger.

Secure an area
to kill any remaining enemy soldiers in the vicinity.

Security contractors
mercenaries hired as professional soldiers – or the agencies
that provide them.

Servicing a target

killing.

Spontaneous energetic disassembly

an explosion.

Surgical strike

a military attack; surgery is generally
considered beneficial … such a strike is
consequently a remedy for some
'illness' (as perceived by those
perpetrating the strike), and therefore
for the good of all concerned.

Tactical

an action taken under pressure – a 'tactical regrouping'
being a forced retreat.

Take a walk

to defect.

Take out

to render ineffective, most likely by killing.

Terminate with extreme prejudice

to kill.

Terrorist

armed political rebel.

Unclassified

not classified – that is, not secret, but carrying the
implication that the natural state of information is to be
classified. Unclassified information is therefore information
that has been made accessible to the privileged few.

Unlawful combatants

detainees denied prisoner-of-war status. The US Secretary of
Defense, Donald Rumsfeld, announced in 2002 that prisoners
at Guantanamo Bay would not be viewed in legal terms as
prisoners of war, but as 'unlawful combatants'. As such, 'they

do not have any rights under the Geneva Convention'. It was not until June 2004 that this categorization was overturned.

Vertically deployed anti-personnel devices

bombs, usually dropped from the air.

Vigilance

spying; also, in a totalitarian state, informing on fellow citizens to the authorities.

Wet work

assassination (see also the section on Killing).

Zero tolerance

implies, in a government, a policy of not putting up with crime or poverty or anything else that the electorate complains of, and acting with speed and efficiency in ridding the nation of these problems. Not as dramatic or as efficient as it sounds. The phrase is usually heard in the mouths of politicians and figures in authority as they announce that they will not put up with whatever they are putting up with (violence in schools, street crime, etc.). 'Zero' has a stylishly terse sound to it, making the phrase definite (no woolly politician talk here) and businesslike. Taken literally, however, the phrase could mean 'tolerating nothing' – which in a society that quite rightly calls for people to be more tolerant towards each other, does sound somewhat odd.

To do with mind, body and everyday life

Social life is spattered with euphemism. Sometimes this is a conscious linguistic choice, as in our use of polite or 'politically correct' terms when speaking to someone who might in one way or another be different from us – we also consciously use euphemism when describing or interacting with someone who might be behaving unusually, or who has done something we might view with disapproval or distaste. On other occasions we use euphemism unconsciously – it might be the only acceptable term, or the term that everyone uses, and we therefore employ it without thinking. Although in its extreme forms euphemism can be risible – over-elaborate political correctness, ridiculous refinements and so on – it has its uses in avoiding hurting people's feelings, avoiding causing offence and, sometimes, in actively encouraging people, through the avoidance of apparent condemnation or mockery.

One of the trickiest areas is that of race. You don't use euphemisms in referring to different races – it is not an area where euphemism is needed. Neither should it be necessary to refer to a person by their racial characteristics or culture, but sometimes there is no option – when the person in question is a complete stranger, for instance, and race is used in a descriptive capacity. So many different terms have developed over the centuries for different races that you have to be careful not to refer inadvertently to someone by a term which has become offensive. There are many pitfalls, especially in a nation where so many racial and social backgrounds are integrated. And everything depends on how a term is used and by whom – if you are a West Indian, for example, you and your mates might quite happily refer to yourselves as 'niggahs' (the pronunciation deliberate), but the word 'nigger' is socially taboo, especially so when used by a white person. To make things trickier, there are terms that are now taboo which were once acceptable.

A number of the terms listed here are dysphemisms or cacophemisms – or, at any rate, insulting slang – and apply to people from many countries. The 'insult' is often lightly meant, however: it is an international sport to speak offensively of other nationalities, and these terms are usually used flippantly with no other intent than that. Similarly, a number of the terms listed are jocular racial slang generated by the racial group itself, and used as an 'in joke' and cultural identifier, always in a light-hearted manner.

People are also self-conscious and touchy about other social aspects – not just regarding culture and appearance, but anything that makes individuals different from the majority (even though individualism is also a perceived ambition, and there are those who might seek to make themselves different by artificial means, such as dying their hair an unlikely colour); thus any disability requires sensitive treatment, and even temporary conditions (pregnancy, illness, drunkenness, etc.) have given rise to a raft of alternative terms. A different background, different-coloured skin, different shapes and sizes, different ideas as to what is edible … all are seen as excuses for saying something rude or, conversely, are reasons to worry that we might inadvertently offend someone with our words. Our daily conversation is spattered with evasion and circumlocution as we stumble along through a mass of supporting ers and ums. Everyday life requires verbal agility – below are just a few examples of the gymnastic feats we flaunt.

Appearance and race

Aboriginals
the indigenous people of Australia. The shortened form, 'Abo', has been considered offensive since the 1950s.

African-American
in the States, this is the current preferred term for a black person; over the last decades the approved term was 'black', followed by 'Negro', then 'black' (again), followed by 'Afro-American', and then 'person of colour' (not 'coloured person').

Afro-Saxon
young whites who 'act black'.

Albino
what American blacks call whites.

Altogether, in the
naked – though it is unclear as to why; 'altogether' means 'whole' or 'complete', yet the implication is not that you are less complete when fully dressed.

Ample
fat.

As Allah/God made him/her
naked.

Beanpole
used to describe someone tall and thin, usually jokily.

Below medium height
a polite (politically correct) way of saying 'short'.

Big-boned
overweight.

Big-nose

Chinese term for a Caucasian white; in the US it is a derogatory name for a Jew.

Birthday suit

naked.

Bog trotter

offensive British term for Irish.

Challenged

different – and implicitly unable to become like everybody else.

Chinaman

a pejorative term for a Chinese man.

Chink

a pejorative term for a Chinese person.

Chocolate drop

pejorative term for a black person.

Chubby

fat.

Classic proportions

fat.

Coconut

derogatory term for a black who is thought to be 'acting white' (whatever that may mean) – because a coconut is brown (actually, it is green but that does not seem to come into it) on the outside, white on the inside. In New Zealand it can mean Pacific Islander, presumably because the coconut is a main and versatile crop of that place.

Colour

applied to racial issues.

Convict

Aboriginal pejorative for a white Australian, whom they also call 'criminal' (from the eighteenth- and nineteenth-century transportation of European convicts to penal colonies in Australia).

Demographically correct

containing the 'correct' proportion of people of different race, i.e. in a small sample, the proportions of different racial groups contained therein should reflect the wider proportions in society itself (as well as balancing all the other features that are, or should be, taken into account in such surveys, in order to make them fully representative – e.g. gender).

Didicoi/y

dialect term for gypsy.

Differently sized

fat or obese.

Differently weighted

fat or obese. Interestingly, not used to mean 'over skinny'.

Eskimo

considered a pejorative term as it is thought to be the name the Algonquin people of North America gave to the Arctic peoples, believed to mean 'eaters of raw flesh' (but others say it means 'speaking a different language'); the more specific terms, Inuit, Aleut, etc. are preferred.

Ethnic

nowadays this tends to mean 'non-indigenous', often belonging to a non-Western cultural tradition. (Its actual meaning is 'of people having a common national or cultural tradition'.) An 'ethnic minority' is a group of people differing ethnically from the main population.

FBI

'foreign-born Irish' – an American term for Irish immigrants to the US who walk into well-paid white-collar jobs.

First Nations
  accepted Canadian term for the indigenous people
  (otherwise known as 'Indians', a term they do not care for)

Follicularly challenged
  bald (you might reasonably wonder what would challenge a
  follicle, and why).

Foreign Devil
  East Asian term for a white person. See also 'round eyes'.

Fritz
  British and French derisive name for a German.

Frog or froggie
  British pejorative term for a French
  person, because they eat frogs' legs.

F**koff
  French name for a particular kind of
  British youth (obviously not a friendly
  one).

Ghost
  in China, applied to foreigners, particularly the Japanese;
  white (Caucasian) people are called 'white ghosts' (which is
  strange as many northern Chinese have much whiter skin
  than many Europeans).

Greasy wop
  offensive name for an Italian or other Mediterranean
  person. 'Greasy' possibly because of the fashion for hair oil;
  see also 'wop'.

Groundskeeper Willie
  a Scotsman – from a character in *The Simpsons*.

Gyppo
  (UK only) derogatory term for gypsy; in the Second World
  War Allied armies sometimes called Egyptians 'gyppos'; it
  was generally meant affectionately.

Heinz 57

someone of indeterminate racial or national origin.

Homely

plain, ugly.

Horizontally challenged

fat (surely satirical).

Ice mutant

derogatory term for a white person.

In the buff

naked; 'buff' being the bare skin.

Indian

properly, a person from India; when used to refer to Native Americans, the term is considered offensive, as they are indigenous to America and not to India.

Indigenous people

Native Americans – as used in the United States.

Kiwi

a New Zealander, from the bird; not generally considered offensive, and used by New Zealanders themselves.

Limey

US term for a British person – from the days when British sailors ate limes to prevent scurvy.

Mature figure

middle-aged and bordering on being fat, generally of a woman.

Melanin-enriched

black.

Mick/Mickey

an Irishman, sometimes considered pejorative.

Mohammedan

a Muslim; causes offence because it would seem to imply that Muslims worship Muhammad.

Native Americans

indigenous people of the Americas; this term is much preferred to all the others sometimes bandied about (for example, 'American Indians', 'Red Indians', etc.).

Negro

Originally the name given by early Europeans to the people of Africa south of the Sahara, it derives ultimately from the Latin for 'black', *niger*. Until the 1960s, it was considered the proper term to use to describe a black person (as long as, when written, it had a capital N), but fell out of favour, considered at the best old-fashioned, otherwise insulting. Its derivative below, with its connotations of slavery and terrible abuse, is probably the reason for its decline in acceptability.

Nigger

taboo (it derives from a word meaning nothing worse than 'black', but its historical usage is what gives offence): a black person; sometimes also applied to other non-white peoples. Although, among themselves, some black people are happy to refer to themselves as 'niggahs' (and in so doing 'reclaim' the word with dignity), it is considered extremely offensive – so much so that in 1999 a member of the Mayor of Washington's staff had to resign, following an outcry when, at a private meeting, he quite correctly and innocently used the wholly unrelated word 'niggardly' (parsimonious); the critics' niggle probably caused much sniggering in some quarters. Thus is a word unfairly denigrated – the latter a word to which they perhaps should take exception, as it could be translated as 'painted black'.

No oil painting

ugly.

N-word

see 'nigger' (see above).

Oreo

a black person who 'acts white'; someone of black and white descent. An Oreo is a chocolate cookie with a white filling.

Oriental

as a noun, this means someone from the Far East; it is considered offensive as it is properly an adjective that is applied to objects not people.

Osama

pejorative term for an Arab, after the leader of the terrorist organization al-Qaeda, Osama Bin Laden.

Paddy

an Irishman, the diminutive of 'Patrick', a popular Irish name. Often used pejoratively.

Paki

a Pakistani; pejorative.

Person of the coloured persuasion

pompous (or mocking) genteelism for 'a black person'.

Pom, Pommy

(Australian) derisive but not always unaffectionate term for a British person; might be from the rhyming slang: 'immigrant/pomegranate', or the rhyming phrase 'immigrant, Jimmy Grant, pommygrant'. There are also suggestions that it could have come from '*P*risoner *o*f His/Her *M*ajesty' (British convict transportation to Australia took place between 1788 and 1853).

Prod

Protestant – a mainly Catholic Irish term, especially Northern Ireland.

Puppy fat

fatness in a child; the implication is that the child will grow out of their extra pounds – and children do when it is genuine puppy fat; sadly, however, these days the excess weight is all too often obesity.

Quantitatively challenged

fat (satirical use of political correctness).

Red devil/red hair

Chinese terms for a white person (from the hair colour).

Red Indian

used in Britain to differentiate between 'American Indians' and the people of India; the term is considered very offensive by Native Americans.

Redskin

Native American (also pejorative).

Round eyes

Asian term for a white person.

Sartorially challenged

badly dressed (the political correctness is ironic).

Skip

Aborigine term for a white Australian of British birth – from the television show *Skippy the Bush Kangaroo*.

Slant-eye, Slit-eye, etc.

an Asian person, so called by whites.

Snow Flake

a white person – a term used by US blacks.

Spade

you can call a spade a spade, but not a black person – this is considered an offensive term; from the ace of spades, which is a black card.

Spare tyre

roll of fat around the waist.

Starkers

stark naked.

Taffy

a derogatory term for a Welshman, probably deriving from the popular Welsh name Dafydd (David); possibly taken into use because of the old nursery rhyme which starts 'Taffy was a Welshman, Taffy was a thief'.

Towelhead

derogatory term for an Arab.

Traveller

one who follows a gypsy's life.

Vertically challenged

politically correct for 'short' (allegedly – who has heard anyone in the street refer to a short person as 'vertically challenged', other than satirically?).

Visually challenging

suggested substitute for 'ugly'.

WASP

White Anglo-Saxon Protestant (originally a shorthand term in sociology); not particularly offensive.

Well-built

fat.

White bread

middle-class white person.

Without a stitch

naked (clothes traditionally consisting of fabric and stitches).

Wog

a deeply offensive term for 'black person'. Its derivation is uncertain – some suggest it is an acronym for one or more of the following phrases: '**W**esternized **O**riental **G**entleman' (a patronizing phrase); '**W**orking **o**n **G**overnment Service', from the shirts of Egyptian workers building the Suez Canal (but one questions whether they would have had such shirts in the 1860s); or even the insulting '**W**ily **O**riental **G**entleman'. Yet these suggestions do not seem very likely. The other contender for the term's original source is 'golliwog', which probably derives in turn from *The Adventures of Two Dutch Dolls*, a children's book by Bertha Upton and her daughter, Florence Kate, published in 1895. One of the characters in the book, the gallant Golliwogg, is clearly based upon a black ragdoll Florence was given as a child in New York – at that time in the States ragdolls made to look like black minstrels were popular. Where the Uptons originally got the name from is also cause for speculation – it could come from the old word for tadpole (pollywog), which seems plausible, given that the book's illustrations show the doll's head as much larger than the rest of its body. 'Pollywog' also seems to have been a slang term for 'an inexperienced sailor', and as many crews were recruited from eastern ports, this too seems a plausible origin.

'Wogs begin at Calais'

this phrase is from an attack upon Churchill in the House of Commons in 1945, during a debate on Burma. MP George Wigg announced: 'The Honourable gentleman and his friends think they [the Burmese] are all "wogs". Indeed, the Right Honourable Member for Woodford [Churchill] thinks that the "wogs" begin at Calais.' Wigg was essentially accusing Churchill of both parochialism and racism.

Wop

offensive term for an Italian (sometimes also applied to other Mediterranean people); its derivation is uncertain – some suggest it is a xenophobic acronym, coined at the time of mass Italian immigration into the United States, i.e. '*W*ith*O*ut *P*assport', '*W*ith*O*ut *P*apers', '*W*ithout *O*fficial *P*apers'. The word's earliest appearance in a dictionary, however, was as 'wap' – which supports the stronger theory that it derives from *guappa*, Italian for 'thug'. However, given the pronunciation, it is even more likely to have derived from the Spanish *guapo* ('handsome, dashing, braggart, dandy'), a term the Spanish applied derisively to the Italian men who, in the nineteenth century, came to Spain to work in the vineyards, and whose good looks delighted the Spanish women. The term could easily have been picked up in Europe by British and American travellers.

Yid

a Jewish person; a pejorative term derived from the word 'Yiddish', the language used by European Jews, which is essentially a mixture of German and Hebrew.

The body, age and other challenges

Ableism

discrimination against or insensitivity to those who are physically or mentally handicapped/disabled/impaired (delete as your PC persuasion decrees).

Accouchement

time of giving birth – a French euphemism, so a genteelism as well as a euphemism in English.

Active

used to describe an old or physically disabled person who is not impaired or restricted by that physical state, and lives a full life.

Aurally challenged

deaf, or hard of hearing.

Big C, the

cancer – a word that still borders on the taboo for many. Nowadays, it is rare for people to use euphemisms for illnesses, except sometimes for venereal diseases (themselves now usually called sexually transmitted diseases, or STDs), which also turn up in various guises in literature or biography. Even diseases such as HIV and Aids – though, like cancer, seen as death sentences – are called by acronyms for the sake of brevity and simplicity, rather than for euphemistic reasons.

Blue rinse

a particular kind of old woman – or, as she'd prefer, lady. So called after the popular hairstyle for women of that generation.

Bun in the oven

pregnant, a cosy euphemism.

Catch a packet

to contract a sexually transmitted disease.

Certain condition

to be in one of these is to be pregnant – a Victorian euphemism.

... Challenged

lacking some feature that is considered a standard requirement (for example, hair on the head, height) or having some disability, from slight to serious (plumpness, say, to total paralysis). It has become something of a catch-all phrase for those seeking to be politically correct, for those wishing to make fun of political correctness at its most silly, and also for those seeking an ironic euphemism (e.g. 'parentally challenged' for 'bastard' – but 'bastard' meaning a thoroughly nasty person).

Clapham

gonorrhoea, which is often referred to as just 'the clap'; from Clapham Common, once a haunt of prostitutes.

Communicable disease

that is, a sexually transmitted disease; it is also used of other communicable diseases, however – usually serious ones such as meningitis. One could argue that all contagious, indeed infectious diseases, for example the common cold, could be described as communicable. A rather broad euphemism.

Crinkly

'old' as an adjective, or an old person; to go with 'wrinkly'.

Cupid's measles

a euphemism for syphilis, from a time when there was no proper cure for it and so, maybe decades after contraction, it could end horribly for the sufferer; literature contains numerous references to the madness which often accompanied the sufferer's last weeks.

Differently able

used to describe someone suffering a disability, and therefore different from those who have no disabilities; the implication that they have some 'different' ability is baffling. Some prefer to use 'physically challenged'.

Disabled

this word – meaning not 'rendered incapable' but 'with some kind of physical or mental limitation' – replaced 'handicapped' (which itself replaced 'invalid' and before that the harsher 'crippled': we tend to be crippled or handicapped by our circumstances these days). In some places, 'disabled' has now given way to 'differently able' or 'physically challenged'. According to signs, some inanimate objects can be disabled: we have, for example, 'disabled toilets' and 'disabled exits'.

Dose

of, for instance, gonorrhoea (see 'Clapham').

Drury Lane ague

a sexually transmitted disease; Drury Lane used to be a haunt of prostitutes.

Emmas, the

rhyming slang from 'Emma Freud/haemorrhoids'. A contemporary linguistic creation.

Enceinte

French for pregnant, therefore refined.

Family planning

contraception – chemists and supermarkets have shelves labelled 'family planning', but what is actually meant is 'family prevention'.

Family way, in the

they didn't plan it in the sense given above.

Feminine complaint

menstruation or other conditions specific to women, which therefore often embarrass men.

French pox

syphilis (also called 'French ache', 'French disease', 'French fever', etc.) – the disease is thought to have been introduced to the rest of Europe by the French. However, in English, much that is considered immoral, illegal, bogus, etc., is prefixed 'French', for all that the French are seen, by some, as the epitome of refinement and elegance.

Golden years

old age – 'golden': does that mean something to look forward to?

Hard of hearing

deaf – or unable to hear well.

Hearing-impaired

either totally deaf or unable to hear well.

Impaired

see 'challenged'.

In pod/calf/foal/pup, etc.

pregnant – which condition apparently turns a woman into an animal, and usually a farm animal at that.

In the club

pregnant, from 'in the pudding club', most probably because of the roundness both pregnancy and puddings assume.

Inconvenienced

in some places, notably the US, this is taking over from 'impaired' – for example, you might be 'visually inconvenienced' rather than blind.

Interesting condition, in an

a Victorian euphemism, now usually employed jocularly, to mean pregnant.

Invalid

nowadays 'not valid', though still used to refer to someone who is ill. No longer used in reference to disability.

Mature

old, with the implication of wisdom brought on by the years.

Optically challenged

blind or with poor eyesight.

Physically challenged

physically impaired, see 'disabled'.

Preggers

pregnant.

Roman spring

an elderly (or middle-aged) person taking a young lover (what would these days be called a 'toy boy'). An allusion to Roman spring festivals celebrating fertility. The film *The Roman Spring of Mrs Stone*, based on Tennessee Williams's 1950 novel of the same title, popularized the phrase.

Sandy McNabs

rhyming slang for 'crabs' – crab- or pubic lice, usually transmitted sexually.

Senior citizen

an old person, replaces 'Old Age Pensioner' as the 'official', proper term.

Senior moment

a moment of forgetfulness, generally used ironically.

Social disease

a sexually transmitted disease, a Victorian euphemism.

Spanish gout

syphilis – see also 'French pox': foreigners have a lot to answer for!

Spastic

Not a euphemism but a word that has fallen into disrepute. A spastic person was someone suffering from a form of cerebral palsy characterized by spasms. It came to be used as a general insult applied to anything or anybody considered not to be working efficiently. Nowadays a person suffering from that form of paralytic disease has to be contented – like so many other disparate people – with 'labels' such as 'physically challenged'.

Sunset years

the 'golden years', but rather more specific in its implication that the day – life – is soon to end.

... Syndrome

meaning a characteristic group of symptoms, but applied to any medical condition of which people are somewhat wary.

Twilight home

where those people in their golden and sunset years are sent, an old people's home.

Vertically challenged

short.

Visually impaired

blind; but if this piece of political correctness were taken literally, it should also mean 'having poor eyesight'.

Wrinkly

old, an old person (see also 'crinkly').

The mind, drunkenness and further challenges

Aled up/beered up

drunk.

Backward

very stupid, unable to reach a basic level of education; see also 'mentally challenged'.

Balance of mind disturbed

an official phrase to indicate temporary insanity – which therefore excuses the actions of the person to whom it is applied, or alleviates the criminality or sinfulness of those actions. It is in fact less vague than 'temporary insanity', because it has the clinical suggestion of 'chemical imbalance of the brain'.

Bananas

mad – a phrase not taken too seriously, but still with a touch of hysteria.

Barking

mad – possibly from the excitable behaviour of barking dogs. An amusing extension is mentioned by R. W. Holder in his wonderful *Oxford Dictionary of Euphemisms*: he cites 'East Ham' for 'mad' – East Ham being one stop short of Barking on the London underground. To be 'East Ham' means that one is slightly less crazy than 'barking mad' – rather like Hamlet's 'but mad north-north-west'; satisfyingly, East Ham is south-east of Barking!

Bats

... in the belfry, i.e mind – mad, but like 'bananas' and 'barking', rarely anything to be worried about, not genuine insanity.

Behaviourally challenged

used to refer to someone guilty of criminal behaviour.

Bender, on a

a serious bout of alcoholic drinking, with the implication that the person is determined to get very drunk indeed.

Black dog

melancholia – a period of gloominess, or of depression.

Blind/blinder

like 'bender'.

Blotto

drunk, even very drunk.

Brahms

rhyming slang – 'Brahms and Liszt/pissed' ('pissed' being a slang term for 'drunk', because excessive drinking means excessive urination).

Burra peg

a large measure of alcoholic drink (from the days of the

Raj); chota peg is a small measure (but then they probably drank more of those to make up the shortfall).

Caned

drunk, possibly from 'can' (as in 'of beer'), or maybe from how a person feels after having drunk himself stupid. In more recent times, 'caned' has come to be more regularly used to describe one's intoxicated state after smoking marijuana, rather than from drinking – though the two meanings are still somewhat interchangeable at the time of writing.

Cerebrally challenged

risible politically correct euphemism for 'stupid'.

Certifiable

sometimes replaced by 'sectionable' – refers to someone whose mental stability is so precarious that they could be certified insane and forcibly kept in a mental institution.

Chemically affected

incapacitated by drugs or alcohol.

Convivial

generally meaning 'lively and sociable', it might be applied to a person who spends much time in a pub or bar and therefore much time more or less drunk.

Developmental

vague term to suggest that somewhere along the line a person's intellectual and behavioural capacities have failed to develop – i.e. they are stupid and/or badly behaved.

Dippy

slightly mad, 'not all there'.

Dipso

dipsomaniac, one who drinks (alcohol) to excess.

Disparate impact

vague US term to mean a difference in ability, intelligence, and so on.

Disturbed

mentally abnormal.

Doolally

a bit mad; a distortion of Deolali, a town near Mumbai (Bombay), where British soldiers of the Raj used to await repatriation; idleness, the hot sun and boredom all went towards the soldiers becoming a bit 'touched in the head' – dippy, dotty, loopy …

Down syndrome

universally and rightly used term for what used to be called 'Mongolism'; 'syndrome' (see section on the Body) is a useful word. The syndrome is named after Dr John Langdon Down (1828–96) who studied the condition.

Dumb down, to

to make simpler – that is, to descend to the lowest level, and appeal to the lowest common denominator – often an act of despair.

Dutch cheer

alcoholic drink (which gives 'Dutch courage' – courage that you only have when alcoholically intoxicated).

Fruitcake

mad – as 'nutty as a fruitcake' ('nutty' itself being another term meaning mad).

Funny

not that funny – mentally unstable.

Half cut

drunk (also half cooked, half gone, half seas, etc.).

Hammered

drunk – possibly from the wonky vision, slurred speech and unsteady walk that heavy drinking causes: the effects would be much similar had one actually been hit on the head with a hammer.

Happy/merry
drunk – but still cheerful and reasonably *compos mentis*.

Hollow legs
able to drink vast amounts of alcohol; and to walk even having drunk copiously.

Imbibe
to drink (and remain genteel).

Indisposed
suffering from a hangover.

Indulge, to
to drink alcohol; to over-indulge is to get drunk, unless it is on food in which case it means to eat yourself sick.

Inebriated
genteelly drunk.

Intellectually challenged
stupid or of low intelligence. Like 'mentally challenged' it ought to mean 'faced with a difficult puzzle'.

Kraepelin's syndrome
this term (named after the German psychiatrist Emil Kroeplin) is now taking preference over 'schizophrenia' ('split mind'), a word which frightens people, and is in any case an inaccurate description of the mental disorder; 'syndrome' (see section on the Body) – a usefully vague and fashionable word.

Late developer
not too clever, but with the implied hope that the person will eventually blossom. Can also be applied to those with slow or delayed physical development during adolescence, though in such instances the term is not euphemistic.

Learning difficulties

if you have these you're unable to keep up in class – but the term is also used of those who are what used to be called 'mentally handicapped', now perhaps 'mentally challenged'?

Legless

very drunk – so drunk that you are unable to walk.

Loopy

mentally abnormal, a bit strange.

Mellow

drunk or on the way to being so. Applied to 'chilled out', relaxed drunkenness rather than lively or high-spirited intoxication.

Mental illness

insanity.

Mentally challenged

suffering from a mental illness; or of low intelligence.

Mozart

rhyming slang for drunk, for those who can't remember the name 'Brahms'.

Nervous breakdown

mental illness – could be a bout of depression or schizophrenia, for instance.

No Einstein/genius

not academic, not too clever (with the implication that too much is being asked of the person in question).

Not a great reader

illiterate.

Not quite right

of very low intelligence, or mentally ill.

Not the sharpest tool in the shed

actually rather stupid.

Nuts

mad, 'wrong in the head'; the person might be 'a nutter', 'a nutcase', 'nutty' or 'off his nut'. Used fairly jocularly, e.g. to describe someone who takes risks – for example, if someone does a bungee jump, you might describe them as 'a nutter'.

On the bottle

drinking seriously – alcoholic.

On the wagon

determined avoidance of alcoholic drink; possibly from the days of the early Prohibition, when anyone who had sworn abstinence from alcohol (and would presumably be drinking largely water from then on) was said to have 'climbed aboard the water wagon' (the water on the wagon was in fact not for drinking, but for damping down the dust on the roads, which made it pretty unpalatable); later shortened to 'on the wagon'.

One over the eight/one too many

having had too much to drink. The former phrase comes from the fact that there are eight pints to the gallon.

Out to lunch

mentally unstable.

Paralytic

extremely drunk, 'legless'.

Pie-eyed

very drunk, unable to focus.

Pissed

very drunk (see also 'Brahms').

Variously appears as 'pissed as a newt', 'pissed out of his/her skull', 'pissed to the eyeballs', and so on. In the US it means 'angry', like the British phrase 'pissed off'.

Plastered

very drunk – perhaps paralytically so, as if encased in plaster, and thus dispossessed of physical coordination.

Psycho

mentally ill and potentially violent.

Put away

to drink, quaff.

Round the bend

mad, mentally unstable.

Sandwich short of a picnic

mentally abnormal, of low intelligence or plain loopy; variations include 'penny/pennies short of a shilling' etc.

Screw loose

mentally abnormal – head not properly screwed on.

Sectionable

see 'certifiable'.

Sheets to the wind

usually three or four sheets, meaning mildly drunk; a sheet is a rope that ties a sail to a spar – when several are loose, the ship is in some disarray.

Sloshed

drunk – drink is sloshing around inside the person in question.

Sozzled

drunk; like 'squiffy' or 'tiddly' (see entries below), the word has an amused, tolerant tone – drunk but not unpleasantly so.

Spifflicated

drunk (and a difficult word to say when so).

Squiffy

drunk, literally 'askew, lopsided'. See also 'sozzled'.

Tanked/tanked up

drunk – full of alcohol.

Tiddly

merry – from the rhyming slang 'tiddly-wink/drink'.

Tipsy
'tiddly'.

Tired and emotional
drunk, politely put. Famously used – to the delight of
Private Eye magazine – of a certain politician.

Touched
drunk; or if ' … in the head', mentally unsound.

Unbalanced/unhinged
mentally unsound.

Under the table
very drunk (and has slid down under the table). Also used
when challenging people to drinking competitions, as in 'I
could drink you under the table' (the implication being that
the challenger would remain upright, and thus be the
'competitor' best able to 'hold their drink').

Under the weather
unwell.

Upstairs
to do with the head or mind.

Wants for some pence in the shilling
see 'sandwich short of a picnic'.

Worse for wear
drunk.

Everyday genteelisms, evasions, circumlocutions and prevarications

Ass

originally a euphemism for 'arse' (buttocks),
which came about because, while 'arse' had
taboo sexual connotations, a donkey did

not – so 'arse' for 'buttocks' became 'ass'; usage wore off in Britain (though most of the time the animal is still called a 'donkey'), but not in the United States, where it still means 'arse'. In the UK when we call someone an 'ass' we are telling them that they are foolish.

Assist

to help – but 'assist' sounds more important. 'May I be of assistance?' is both genteelism and circumlocution for what can be more succinctly put as 'Can I help you?' (Or, if we're to be proper, 'May I help you?').

Backside

your rump, the part that goes over the fence last, your bottom, your bum (a contraction of 'bottom'), buttocks, butt (mainly in the US) and so on; there are many terms, jokey, evasive or 'refined', for a part of the anatomy that is more laughed-at than any other.

Behind

your 'behind' is your bottom, but sounds more refined.

Bend sinister

a suggestion of illegitimacy (heraldic term).

Burger bum

a very wide bottom – usually attached to an obese person and for which over-consumption of burgers is blamed.

Buy into

a stylish phrase used instead of 'agree with', generally in the negative: 'I don't buy into his argument.'

By-blow

illegitimate child.

Child of sin

illegitimate child – see also 'love child'.

Couch

the genteel word for sofa. The couch is usually in the

'lounge', and those who sit upon it use 'serviettes' and put 'preserve' on their bread (see relevant entries below).

Derrière

literally 'behind' (see above); the use of French words is thought to be a sign of refinement.

Dysfunctional family

used to mean a broken home (i.e. a home with a parental split), or at least a family that does not get on. Two families that are described as dysfunctional are the fictitious one of the Simpsons and the real-life one of singer Ozzy Osbourne (his family relationships are well documented in the hit reality-TV show *The Osbournes*). The first could not be a closer, more loving family, while the latter has its moments of madness and roaring rows, but is nevertheless full of eccentric affection and mutual support. So what is dysfunctional now? Interestingly enough, the popularity of *The Osbournes* – together with its accompanying merchandise bearing the slogan 'The Parents You Wish You Had' – has made having a so-called dysfunctional family practically desirable.

Economical with the truth

lying – or at least conveying an untrue version of events by missing out some important facts. The phrase goes back a couple of centuries, but was brought into prominence in the 1980s by the UK Cabinet Secretary, Sir Robert Armstrong, who used the phrase during a trial arising from an alleged breach of confidence (by Peter Wright, a former security agent, in his book *Spycatcher*).

Edifice

building, but one which sounds more important.

Embroidering the truth

lying.

Enormity

adopted as a stylish word but frequently – usually – used wrongly to mean 'enormousness', rather than its actual definition of 'extreme gravity or wickedness'.

Enquire

to ask – but a more fashionable word; sometimes the term is used facetiously, as when you find a burglar in your front room and ask of him, 'May I enquire what you are doing here?'

Expectorate

to spit; a genteelism because the word is long and not Anglo-Saxon.

Feel

know – an evasion or circumlocution: 'I feel you don't like me' instead of 'I know you don't like me', means that 'you' can deny it.

Fortuitously

adopted as a stylish alternative to 'fortunately' – although, strictly speaking, it means 'coming or happening by a lucky chance'.

Four-letter word

a euphemism to cover a number of taboo words, that conveniently all happen to be made up of four letters. Expediently, it confuses young children as a great many other words also have only four letters.

Gender

first and foremost a grammatical term but it has come to mean 'sex', as in 'What sex – er, gender – is your baby?', in case the word 'sex' gives the wrong idea. 'Sex' itself has now become interchangeable with the term 'sexual intercourse', so people are reluctant to employ 'sex' in its other capacities, as it now summons up that physical intimacy and act: not always wholly appropriate in some contexts.

Gluteus maximus

a jokey euphemism for bottom; the *gluteus maximus* is the largest of the three muscles that form each buttock.

I am hearing you

'I think I understand what you're on about but I don't agree.' Usually used to make the speaker appear as though they are taking on board their opponent's points (i.e. in an argument); generally the opposite is true.

I hate to say

... but I am going to, and might even enjoy doing so: a softening-up before doling out harsh criticism.

I know

evasive circumlocution to begin a statement: the term 'even though' might be more accurate in these contexts, but comes across as too harsh, as in 'I know you're tired, but could you stay on and finish the job?'

I see where you're coming from

I understand what you're saying and the stance you are taking, but I don't agree with you.

I should

implicit is 'but I am not going to'.

Interesting

as a genteelism or evasion it is a way of saying you neither understand it nor like it.

Lady dog

genteel term for 'bitch'; or perhaps out of consideration for the dog's feelings.

Let's agree to differ

... but I know that I am right and you are wrong.

Like

a filler word, which generally highlights an evasion or stalling of some sort, but could also just be a sign of inarticulacy or an inability to think (used in sentences such as, 'and it was, like, the tallest building I'd ever seen').

Lingerie

genteelism for underclothes; as it's a French word it suggests rather superior and also rather skimpy, frilly articles (rather than your old, grey 'granny pants'). Used for women's underclothes only.

Lingerie

Lounge

genteel word for sitting room.

Love child

an illegitimate child.

Medical correctness

awkward avoidance of direct reference to taboo illnesses; this has now by and large fallen into desuetude, as however good the intentions were, it led to much distress.

No better than she should be

a genteel way of casting aspersions upon a woman's morals – she is not as good as she should be.

Not sure

an evasion – 'I'm not sure' actually means 'I don't know (… but I want to give the impression that I almost know but am being cautious so as not to mislead)'.

Odour

a genteel smell.

Oh well

implying a slight, or discomfort, silently endured – too bad, that's how it is …

Pardon

much despised as a genteelism when it is used to mean

'What (did you say)?', 'Excuse me', 'Sorry' and so on.
Properly, 'to pardon' is to excuse or forgive someone for
a sin, error or transgression, or to remit the legal
consequences of a conviction (as in releasing someone
from prison).

Partake of

to eat or drink.

Paying guest

a genteel term for 'lodger' – only the unrefined would take
in such riff-raff as lodgers.

Politically incorrect

a politically correct phrase to mean 'rude'.

Porky

from rhyming slang: 'pork pie/lie'; it is more tolerant and
less accusatory than 'lie': 'You told a porky, didn't you?' is
far less judgemental and aggressive than 'You told a lie,
didn't you?' The word can also be used as an adjective,
meaning 'fat'.

Posterior

facetious term for the bottom.

Preserve

genteel word for 'jam' (not as in traffic – though, who
knows, we might come to hear of 'traffic preserves'); the
implication being that a 'preserve' is somehow better than a
'jam', perhaps containing more fruit and purer ingredients.

Prevaricating

avoiding a head-on collision with the truth.

Quality time

the time that a working parent, suddenly struck with guilt –
or possibly faced with a dreary week at work – decides they
should be spending with their children. The phrase was
born in 1980s America, with the idea that it should be
possible for working parents to combine a successful career

with a happy home life. Nowadays the phrase is used more generally and with regards to many personal relationships.

Scope

a charity which was formerly called 'The National Spastics Society', but changed its name when 'spastic' came to be used offensively to mean incompetent or clumsy. This change of title is understandable given our PC society – but why has the organization renamed its clothes banks (themselves not really banks, but usage has made 'bank' the accepted term) 'outdoor donation units'?

Scratch, a little

until comparatively recently, if you were having blood taken for a test you'd be told to expect 'a little prick'; now it's 'a little scratch' (and of course it is not a scratch at all).

Serviette

genteelism for 'napkin', the French being considered more refined (in spite of their 'naughty' image, which has given rise to euphemisms the likes of 'French kissing' and 'French letters').

Sit-upon

genteel, but also mildly jokey term for the bottom.

Spinning a windy

lying.

Sufficient

enough – a genteelism. The refined – or mock-refined – reply when offered some more tea and cake is 'Thank you, but I have had an elegant sufficiency.'

Taxpayer

citizen; a word which ignores those who do not pay taxes, and appeals instead to the pockets of those who do – generally heard in the mouths of politicians: 'Is this what the taxpayers want us to do …?'

Termination
could be a genteelism for 'end'; also used for 'abortion'.
Terminological inexactitude
a Churchillism (term coined by Winston Churchill) – a lie.

Unfortunately
in excusing oneself – employed to mean 'fortunately'
('Unfortunately I met a lion on the way to school and it ate
up all my homework').

Whatever
means – whatever you'd like it to mean; but usually with
the implication 'I can't be bothered to go on talking' –
'whatever you say', 'whatever it might mean', even the
sullen, teenage 'whatever', which probably means
something along the lines of 'shut up and leave me alone'.
Womyn
a neologism – meant to mean 'woman'. The word did not
catch on; neither did the preposterous 'herstory' for
'history', a discipline which has nothing whatsoever to do
with hims and hers.
Wrong side of the blanket, to be born on
to be illegitimate.

You're entitled to your opinion
… but you're wrong.

Conclusion

Many of our verbal expressions, notably euphemisms and similar metaphorical figures of speech, do their utmost to veil our real meaning in our interaction with others. But maybe this book has gone some way in drawing aside that veil for you – perhaps it has shown you why it's not a good idea to name your son Percy; why if a young woman assures you she is 'a working girl', you should be sure you know what she means; perhaps it has taught you that if somebody asks you if you know Dorothy, they do not necessarily mean dear old Dot from down the road. You will now be forewarned to expect the worst if your boss tells you that your job is above your ceiling; and if you're told that a friend is sailing three sheets to the wind, you know that in all likelihood there's little chance they've gone sailing.

In fact, this book may have shown you that nearly every word in the language is, in one way or another, a terminological inexactitude. Which is a part of their magic, and goes towards explaining the power of language. Most of all, however, this book should have afforded you some entertainment and amusement – even if it has been confined to the 'euphemism'.

Useful books and websites

Books

There are surprisingly few full dictionaries of euphemisms; the most comprehensive available is R. W. Holder's *Oxford Dictionary of Euphemisms*, which is more or less an updated version of *The Faber Dictionary of Euphemisms*, which he compiled some ten years before. The following volumes were of interest:

Balistreri, Maggie. *The Evasion-English Dictionary* (Melville House Publishing, Hoboken, New Jersey, 2003)
Berdoll, Linda. *Very Nice Ways to Say Very Bad Things: The Unusual Book of Euphemisms* (Well, There It Is, Del Valle, Texas, 2003)

Holder, R. W. *The Faber Dictionary of Euphemisms* (Faber and Faber Ltd, London, 1989)
Holder, R. W. *Oxford Dictionary of Euphemisms: How Not to Say What You Mean* (Oxford University Press, Oxford, 1995, 2002, 2003)

Spiegl, Fritz. *In-Words and Out-Words* (Elm Tree Books, London, 1987)

Websites

http://en.wikipedia.org/wiki
http://www.answers.com
http://www.askoxford.com
http://www.infoplease.com
http://www.morewords.com
http://www.phrases.org.uk
http://www.prwatch.org
http://www.worldwidewords.org
http://www.earlyrisers.org.au